Selected Poems

Crofts Classics

GENERAL EDITORS

Samuel H. Beer, *Harvard University*
O. B. Hardison, Jr., *Georgetown University*

JOHN KEATS

Selected
Poems

EDITED BY

George H. Ford

UNIVERSITY OF ROCHESTER

Harlan Davidson, Inc.
Arlington Heights, Illinois 60004

Library of Congress Cataloging-in-Publication Data

Keats, 1795–1821.
    Selected poems.

    (Crofts classics)
    Bibliography: p.
    I. Ford, George Harry, 1914–   . II. Title.
PR4832.F6   1985   821′.7   85-25286
ISBN 0-88295-050-9 (pbk.)

Manufactured in the United States of America
    89 88 87   CM   18 19 20 21

CONTENTS

INTRODUCTION

❧

IN A LETTER to his sister, the English novelist George Gissing once remarked: "Of Keats read everything. To like Keats is a test of fitness for understanding poetry, just as to like Shakespeare is a test of general mental capacity." One cannot readily quarrel with Gissing's suggestion. To read *everything* of Keats gives interesting information about the way a poet develops. A reader can watch the stages, month by month, of Keats' groping attempts to embody the conception of poetry early stated in his "Sleep and Poetry" and can trace out the gradual mellowing of his style into the perfection of his best odes and narratives and of the epic, "Hyperion." Yet such a reading, however interesting, also sacrifices something by its emphasis on minor details. Many of the poems in Keats' collected works are experiments, and attract us only as tentative explorations rather than for their intrinsic value. They are also the experiments of a very young writer. It cannot be repeated too often that almost everything this poet wrote was composed before he reached his twenty-fourth birthday, an age at which most poets have written little of any worth. Consequently there is justification for approaching Keats through a volume of selections. The present selections enable the reader to follow out the main outline of Keats' development and yet to concentrate attention on his major achievement.

In his last years at school, John Keats suddenly became keenly interested in reading. His first enthusiasm was for translations of classical literature, and through these he developed a frame of reference from the stories of Greece and Rome upon which he draws extensively in his poems. Later, while he was studying to become a surgeon, his real inclination was for reading poetry, especially that of Spenser, Shakespeare, Milton, and of his own contemporaries Wordsworth, and Leigh Hunt.

The influence of Leigh Hunt is marked in the style of Keats' earlier writings. To avoid stiffness and formality, Hunt recommended a chatty, free-flowing kind of verse. The result is sometimes charming but often simply languid or effete, as can be seen in parts of "Sleep and Poetry" and in a few of the early sonnets. To a diminishing extent, these conventions persist in Keats' poems, even in such works as "Isabella," but his constant effort as he matured was to prune away his "Huntianisms." In "The Eve of St. Agnes," instead of free-flow, there is density and a concentrated richness of expression. And if "Lamia" is sometimes chatty, it is closer to Dryden's masculine talk than to Hunt's languor. "Hyperion," with its echoes of Milton, shows even more clearly Keats' later habit of what he called "loading every rift of the subject with ore."

Together with his reading of Shakespeare, Milton, and other writers, Keats' own experiences contributed to the increased depth of his mature poems. Until 1818, his life had been cheerful and lacking in complexity. The pleasant landscapes of his earlier verse reflect his predominant mood of carefree enjoyment. In 1818, however, a walking tour through Scotland made him acquainted with the more rugged and barren aspects of landscape. It served, as he said, to strengthen his "reach in Poetry." A few months later, the death of his brother from tuberculosis, his own frustrating love affair with Fanny Brawne, and his growing awareness that his career as lover and poet was to be very brief—all combined to make his response to the short-lived beauty about him more sharp and more intricate. "How astonishingly does the chance of leaving the world impress a sense of its natural beauties on us," he wrote in one of his last letters. "Like poor Falstaff, though I do not babble, I think of green fields."

These personal experiences are reflected in his themes:

> Verse, Fame, and Beauty are intense indeed,
> But Death intenser—Death is Life's high meed.

It is the rich juxtaposition of such contrasting themes in Keats' best poems that produces the quality of intensity he sought in art, and it is this effective juxtaposition that some recent critics have praised under the name of "paradox." Certainly the reader who regards "The Eve of St. Agnes" as simply a love poem will miss its point and be bewildered by its final stanzas. For it is a poem of marked contrasts in which love is accentuated by hate, warmth by cold, joy and beauty by death. "The excellence of every art," said Keats, "is its intensity, capable of making all disagreeables evaporate, from their being in close relationship with Beauty and Truth. Examine 'King Lear,' and you will find this exemplified throughout." Keats' own poems can be examined similarly. The "disagreeables" of death and change are usually present. Their evaporation arises from the magic of the poetry itself.

There is much disagreement about the most suitable way of arranging Keats' poems for reading. In the present text, the experiment is made of printing the sonnets separately from the other poems. The aim is both to avoid clutter among the poems and to present the sonnets as representative of Keats' achievement in microcosm. Many readers may prefer to begin with the sonnet section. The section of twenty-one poems and the section of twenty sonnets are each arranged in chronological order. At the end of every selection, dates of composition appear on the left, and dates of first publication on the right. Complete texts are given for all poems except *Endymion*, and the excerpted lines from that poem can be justifiably regarded as a separate unit.

PRINCIPAL DATES IN THE LIFE OF JOHN KEATS

✻

1795   John Keats born in London, October 31st(?).

1803-11   Attended Clarke school, Enfield.

1804   Death of his father, Thomas Keats, stable-keeper.

1810   Death of his mother from tuberculosis.

1811-15   Apprenticed to a surgeon in Edmonton. Began writing.

1815-16   Studied surgery in London. Qualified to practice but preferred career in literature. "Sleep and Poetry" and several sonnets written.

1817   His first volume, *Poems,* published, March. Lived near London with his brothers. Made many friends including Haydon, the painter, and Hunt, the poet.

1818   *Endymion,* his second volume, published, and attacked later by reviewers. His brother George emigrated to Kentucky. After a walking tour through Scotland, he returned to look after his brother Tom, who died in December. Met Fanny Brawne. Began writing early part of *Hyperion* (completed spring 1819).

1819   Winter: "The Eve of St. Agnes" written.
Spring: Wrote most of his major odes. Probably became engaged.
Summer: Visited Isle of Wight. "Lamia" written.
Autumn: Plays written. Illness marked by increasing symptoms of tuberculosis.

1820   Became virtually an invalid. Looked after by friends. Third volume of poems, *Lamia . . . and Other Poems* published, July. To recover health, sailed to Italy, September.

1821   Died in Rome, February 23.

SELECTED POEMS OF JOHN KEATS

❧

Sleep and Poetry

As I lay in my bed slepe full unmete
Was unto me, but why that I ne might
Rest I ne wist, for there n'as erthly wight
[As I suppose] had more of hertis ese
Than I, for I n'ad sicknesse nor disese.

CHAUCER.

WHAT is more gentle than a wind in summer?
What is more soothing than the pretty hummer
That stays one moment in an open flower,
And buzzes cheerily from bower to bower?
What is more tranquil than a musk-rose blowing
In a green island, far from all men's knowing?
More healthful than the leafiness of dales?
More secret than a nest of nightingales?
More serene than Cordelia's countenance?
More full of visions than a high romance? 10
What, but thee Sleep? Soft closer of our eyes!
Low murmurer of tender lullabies!
Light hoverer around our happy pillows!
Wreather of poppy buds, and weeping willows!
Silent entangler of a beauty's tresses!
Most happy listener! when the morning blesses
Thee for enlivening all the cheerful eyes
That glance so brightly at the new sun-rise.

But what is higher beyond thought than thee?
Fresher than berries of a mountain tree? 20
More strange, more beautiful, more smooth, more regal,
Than wings of swans, than doves, than dim-seen eagle?
What is it? And to what shall I compare it?
It has a glory, and naught else can share it:

2 **Hummer** bee

1

The thought thereof is awful, sweet, and holy,
Chasing away all worldliness and folly;
Coming sometimes like fearful claps of thunder,
Or the low rumblings earth's regions under;
And sometimes like a gentle whispering
30 Of all the secrets of some wond'rous thing
That breathes about us in the vacant air;
So that we look around with prying stare,
Perhaps to see shapes of light, aerial lymning,
And catch soft floatings from a faint-heard hymning;
To see the laurel wreath, on high suspended,
That is to crown our name when life is ended.
Sometimes it gives a glory to the voice,
And from the heart up-springs, "Rejoice! rejoice!"
Sounds which will reach the Framer of all things,
40 And die away in ardent mutterings.

No one who once the glorious sun has seen,
And all the clouds, and felt his bosom clean
For his great Maker's presence, but must know
What 'tis I mean, and feel his being glow:
Therefore no insult will I give his spirit,
By telling what he sees from native merit.

O Poesy! for thee I hold my pen
That am not yet a glorious denizen
Of thy wide heaven—Should I rather kneel
50 Upon some mountain-top until I feel
A glowing splendour round about me hung,
And echo back the voice of thine own tongue?
O Poesy! for thee I grasp my pen
That am not yet a glorious denizen
Of thy wide heaven; yet, to my ardent prayer,
Yield from thy sanctuary some clear air,
Smoothed for intoxication by the breath
Of flowering bays, that I may die a death
Of luxury, and my young spirit follow
60 The morning sun-beams to the great Apollo

33 **lymning** delicate painting 58 **bays** laurel trees which symbol-
ize poetic fame because their leaves were woven into garlands to
crown successful poets 60 **Apollo** god of light, youth and beauty,
also associated with music and poetry

Like a fresh sacrifice; or, if I can bear
The o'erwhelming sweets, 'twill bring to me the fair
Visions of all places: a bowery nook
Will be elysium—an eternal book
Whence I may copy many a lovely saying
About the leaves, and flowers—about the playing
Of nymphs in woods, and fountains; and the shade
Keeping a silence round a sleeping maid;
And many a verse from so strange influence
That we must ever wonder how, and whence   70
It came. Also imaginings will hover
Round my fire-side, and haply there discover
Vistas of solemn beauty, where I'd wander
In happy silence, like the clear Meander
Through its lone vales; and where I found a spot
Of awfuller shade, or an enchanted grot,
Or a green hill o'erspread with chequered dress
Of flowers, and fearful from its loveliness,
Write on my tablets all that was permitted,
All that was for our human senses fitted.   80
Then the events of this wide world I'd seize
Like a strong giant, and my spirit teaze
Till at its shoulders it should proudly see
Wings to find out an immortality.

Stop and consider! life is but a day;
A fragile dew-drop on its perilous way
From a tree's summit; a poor Indian's sleep
While his boat hastens to the monstrous steep
Of Montmorenci. Why so sad a moan?
Life is the rose's hope while yet unblown;   90
The reading of an ever-changing tale;
The light uplifting of a maiden's veil;
A pigeon tumbling in clear summer air;
A laughing school-boy, without grief or care,
Riding the springy branches of an elm.

O for ten years, that I may overwhelm
Myself in poesy; so I may do the deed
That my own soul has to itself decreed.
Then will I pass the countries that I see

89 **Montmorenci** waterfall near Quebec city

100 In long perspective, and continually
Taste their pure fountains. First the realm I'll pass
Of Flora, and old Pan: sleep in the grass,
Feed upon apples red, and strawberries,
And choose each pleasure that my fancy sees;
Catch the white-handed nymphs in shady places,
To woo sweet kisses from averted faces,—
Play with their fingers, touch their shoulders white
Into a pretty shrinking with a bite
As hard as lips can make it: till agreed,
110 A lovely tale of human life we'll read.
And one will teach a tame dove how it best
May fan the cool air gently o'er my rest;
Another, bending o'er her nimble tread,
Will set a green robe floating round her head,
And still will dance with ever varied ease,
Smiling upon the flowers and the trees:
Another will entice me on, and on
Through almond blossoms and rich cinnamon;
Till in the bosom of a leafy world
120 We rest in silence, like two gems upcurled
In the recesses of a pearly shell.

And can I ever bid these joys farewell?
Yes, I must pass them for a nobler life,
Where I may find the agonies, the strife
Of human hearts: for lo! I see afar,
O'ersailing the blue cragginess, a car
And steeds with streamy manes—the charioteer
Looks out upon the winds with glorious fear:
And now the numerous tramplings quiver lightly
130 Along a huge cloud's ridge; and now with sprightly
Wheel downward come they into fresher skies,
Tipt round with silver from the sun's bright eyes.
Still downward with capacious whirl they glide;
And now I see them on the green-hill's side
In breezy rest among the nodding stalks.
The charioteer with wond'rous gesture talks
To the trees and mountains; and there soon appear
Shapes of delight, of mystery, and fear,
Passing along before a dusky space

102 **Flora** goddess of flowers **Pan** god of pastures and forests

Made by some mighty oaks: as they would chase 140
Some ever-fleeting music on they sweep.
Lo! how they murmur, laugh, and smile, and weep:
Some with upholden hand and mouth severe;
Some with their faces muffled to the ear
Between their arms; some, clear in youthful bloom,
Go glad and smilingly athwart the gloom;
Some looking back, and some with upward gaze;
Yes, thousands in a thousand different ways
Flit onward—now a lovely wreath of girls
Dancing their sleek hair into tangled curls; 150
And now broad wings. Most awfully intent
The driver of those steeds is forward bent,
And seems to listen: O that I might know
All that he writes with such a hurrying glow.

The visions all are fled—the car is fled
Into the light of heaven, and in their stead
A sense of real things comes doubly strong,
And, like a muddy stream, would bear along
My soul to nothingness: but I will strive
Against all doubtings, and will keep alive 160
The thought of that same chariot, and the strange
Journey it went.

        Is there so small a range
In the present strength of manhood, that the high
Imagination cannot freely fly
As she was wont of old? prepare her steeds,
Paw up against the light, and do strange deeds
Upon the clouds? Has she not shown us all?
From the clear space of ether, to the small
Breath of new buds unfolding? From the meaning
Of Jove's large eye-brow, to the tender greening 170
Of April meadows? Here her altar shone,
E'en in this isle; and who could paragon
The fervid choir that lifted up a noise
Of harmony, to where it aye will poise
Its mighty self of convoluting sound,
Huge as a planet, and like that roll round,
Eternally around a dizzy void?

173 **fervid choir** English poets of the late sixteenth and early
seventeenth centuries

Ay, in those days the Muses were nigh cloyed
With honors; nor had any other care
180   Than to sing out and sooth their wavy hair.

Could all this be forgotten? Yes, a schism
Nurtured by foppery and barbarism,
Made great Apollo blush for this his land.
Men were thought wise who could not understand
His glories: with a puling infant's force
They swayed about upon a rocking horse,
And thought it Pegasus. Ah dismal souled!
The winds of heaven blew, the ocean rolled
Its gathering waves—ye felt it not. The blue
190   Bared its eternal bosom, and the dew
Of summer nights collected still to make
The morning precious: beauty was awake!
Why were ye not awake? But ye were dead
To things ye knew not of,—were closely wed
To musty laws lined out with wretched rule
And compass vile: so that ye taught a school
Of dolts to smooth, inlay, and clip, and fit,
Till, like the certain wands of Jacob's wit,
Their verses tallied. Easy was the task:
200   A thousand handicraftsmen wore the mask
Of Poesy. Ill-fated, impious race!
That blasphemed the bright Lyrist to his face,
And did not know it,—no, they went about,
Holding a poor, decrepid standard out
Marked with most flimsy mottos, and in large
The name of one Boileau!

               O ye whose charge
It is to hover round our pleasant hills!
Whose congregated majesty so fills
My boundly reverence, that I cannot trace
210   Your hallowed names, in this unholy place,
So near those common folk; did not their shames
Affright you? Did our old lamenting Thames

180 **sooth** smooth   181 **schism** breach in the tradition of English
poetry caused by neo-Classical writers   187 **Pegasus** wingèd horse
associated by poets with flights of imagination   206 **Boileau**
French critic (1636-1711) admired by English neo-Classical writers 209 **boundly** bounden

Delight you? Did ye never cluster round
Delicious Avon, with a mournful sound,
And weep? Or did ye wholly bid adieu
To regions where no more the laurel grew?
Or did ye stay to give a welcoming
To some lone spirits who could proudly sing
Their youth away, and die? 'Twas even so:
But let me think away those times of woe: 220
Now 'tis a fairer season; ye have breathed
Rich benedictions o'er us; ye have wreathed
Fresh garlands: for sweet music has been heard
In many places;—some has been upstirred
From out its crystal dwelling in a lake,
By a swan's ebon bill; from a thick brake,
Nested and quiet in a valley mild,
Bubbles a pipe; fine sounds are floating wild
About the earth: happy are ye and glad.

These things are doubtless: yet in truth we've had   230
Strange thunders from the potency of song;
Mingled indeed with what is sweet and strong,
From majesty: but in clear truth the themes
Are ugly clubs, the Poets Polyphemes
Disturbing the grand sea. A drainless shower
Of light is poesy; 'tis the supreme of power;
'Tis might half slumb'ring on its own right arm.
The very archings of her eye-lids charm
A thousand willing agents to obey,
And still she governs with the mildest sway: 240
But strength alone though of the Muses born
Is like a fallen angel: trees uptorn,
Darkness, and worms, and shrouds, and sepulchres

218 **lone spirits** pre-Romantic poets such as Thomas Chatterton
223 **sweet music** poetry of the Romantic period 231 **thunders**
probably ref. to Byron's poetry 234 **Polyphemes** one-eyed giants
of great strength who were armed with "ugly clubs." In Homer's
Odyssey, after one of the Polyphemes had been blinded by the
Greeks, he hurled rocks into the sea in order to sink their ship.
Keats alters this picture slightly by having the "grand sea" dis-
turbed by clubs rather than by rocks. In effect, he is comparing
the indiscriminate handling of themes by some Romantic poets to
the indiscriminate wielding of clubs by the blinded giant in
Homer's story.

Delight it; for it feeds upon the burrs,
And thorns of life; forgetting the great end
Of poesy, that it should be a friend
To sooth the cares, and lift the thoughts of man.

Yet I rejoice: a myrtle fairer than
E'er grew in Paphos, from the bitter weeds
250 Lifts its sweet head into the air, and feeds
A silent space with ever sprouting green.
All tenderest birds there find a pleasant screen,
Creep through the shade with jaunty fluttering,
Nibble the little cuppèd flowers and sing.
Then let us clear away the choking thorns
From round its gentle stem; let the young fawns,
Yeanèd in after times, when we are flown,
Find a fresh sward beneath it, overgrown
With simple flowers: let there nothing be
260 More boisterous than a lover's bended knee;
Nought more ungentle than the placid look
Of one who leans upon a closèd book;
Nought more untranquil than the grassy slopes
Between two hills. All hail delightful hopes!
As she was wont, th' imagination
Into most lovely labyrinths will be gone,
And they shall be accounted poet kings
Who simply tell the most heart-easing things.
O may these joys be ripe before I die.

270 Will not some say that I presumptuously
Have spoken? that from hastening disgrace
'Twere better far to hide my foolish face?
That whining boyhood should with reverence bow
Ere the dread thunderbolt could reach? How!
If I do hide myself, it sure shall be
In the very fane, the light of Poesy:
If I do fall, at least I will be laid
Beneath the silence of a poplar shade;
And over me the grass shall be smooth shaven;
280 And there shall be a kind memorial graven.
But off Despondence! miserable bane!
They should not know thee, who athirst to gain
A noble end, are thirsty every hour.
What though I am not wealthy in the dower

Of spanning wisdom; though I do not know
The shiftings of the mighty winds that blow
Hither and thither all the changing thoughts
Of man: though no great minist'ring reason sorts
Out the dark mysteries of human souls
To clear conceiving: yet there ever rolls   290
A vast idea before me, and I glean
Therefrom my liberty; thence too I've seen
The end and aim of Poesy. 'Tis clear
As anything most true; as that the year
Is made of the four seasons—manifest
As a large cross, some old cathedral's crest,
Lifted to the white clouds. Therefore should I
Be but the essence of deformity,
A coward, did my very eye-lids wink
At speaking out what I have dared to think.   300
Ah! rather let me like a madman run
Over some precipice; let the hot sun
Melt my Dedalian wings, and drive me down
Convulsed and headlong! Stay! an inward frown
Of conscience bids me be more calm awhile.
An ocean dim, sprinkled with many an isle,
Spreads awfully before me. How much toil!
How many days! what desperate turmoil!
Ere I can have explored its widenesses.
Ah, what a task! upon my bended knees,   310
I could unsay those—no, impossible!
Impossible!

    For sweet relief I'll dwell
On humbler thoughts, and let this strange assay
Begun in gentleness die so away.
E'en now all tumult from my bosom fades:
I turn full hearted to the friendly aids
That smooth the path of honour; brotherhood,
And friendliness the nurse of mutual good.
The hearty grasp that sends a pleasant sonnet
Into the brain ere one can think upon it;   320
The silence when some rhymes are coming out;
And when they're come, the very pleasant rout:

303 **Dedalian** of Dedalus, who invented wings of wax and feathers. With these, his son Icarus flew too near the sun. The wax melted and Icarus plunged to his death in the sea.

The message certain to be done to-morrow—
'Tis perhaps as well that it should be to borrow
Some precious book from out its snug retreat,
To cluster round it when we next shall meet.
Scarce can I scribble on; for lovely airs
Are fluttering round the room like doves in pairs;
Many delights of that glad day recalling,
330 When first my senses caught their tender falling.
And with these airs come forms of elegance
Stooping their shoulders o'er a horse's prance,
Careless, and grand—fingers soft and round
Parting luxuriant curls;—and the swift bound
Of Bacchus from his chariot, when his eye
Made Ariadne's cheek look blushingly.
Thus I remember all the pleasant flow
Of words at opening a portfolio.

Things such as these are ever harbingers
340 To trains of peaceful images: the stirs
Of a swan's neck unseen among the rushes:
A linnet starting all about the bushes:
A butterfly, with golden wings broad parted,
Nestling a rose, convulsed as though it smarted
With over pleasure—many, many more,
Might I indulge at large in all my store
Of luxuries: yet I must not forget
Sleep, quiet with his poppy coronet:
For what there may be worthy in these rhymes
350 I partly owe to him—and thus: the chimes
Of friendly voices had just given place
To as sweet a silence, when I 'gan retrace
The pleasant day, upon a couch at ease.
It was a poet's house who keeps the keys
Of pleasure's temple. Round about were hung
The glorious features of the bards who sung
In other ages—cold and sacred busts
Smiled at each other. Happy he who trusts
To clear Futurity his darling fame!
360 Then there were fauns and satyrs taking aim
At swelling apples with a frisky leap

336 **Ariadne** became the wife of Bacchus   354 **poet's** Leigh
Hunt's

*play a role
in generating
poetic mode*

And reaching fingers, 'mid a luscious heap
Of vine-leaves. Then there rose to view a fane
Of liny marble, and thereto a train
Of nymphs approaching fairly o'er the sward:
One, loveliest, holding her white hand toward
The dazzling sun-rise: two sisters sweet
Bending their graceful figures till they meet
Over the trippings of a little child:
And some are hearing, eagerly, the wild   370
Thrilling liquidity of dewy piping.
See, in another picture, nymphs are wiping
Cherishingly Diana's timorous limbs;—
A fold of lawny mantle dabbling swims
At the bath's edge, and keeps a gentle motion
With the subsiding crystal: as when ocean
Heaves calmly its broad swelling smoothness o'er
Its rocky marge, and balances once more
The patient weeds; that now unshent by foam
Feel all about their undulating home.   380

Sappho's meek head was there half smiling down
At nothing; just as though the earnest frown
Of over thinking had that moment gone
From off her brow, and left her all alone.

Great Alfred's too, with anxious, pitying eyes,
As if he always listened to the sighs
Of the goaded world; and Kosciusko's worn
By horrid suffrance—mightily forlorn.
Petrarch, outstepping from the shady green,
Starts at the sight of Laura; nor can wean   390
His eyes from her sweet face. Most happy they!
For over them was seen a free display
Of out-spread wings, and from between them shone
The face of Poesy: from off her throne
She overlooked things that I scarce could tell.
The very sense of where I was might well
Keep Sleep aloof: but more than that there came
Thought after thought to nourish up the flame
Within my breast; so that the morning light

364 **liny** marked with lines   379 **unshent** unspoiled or unsullied
387 **Kosciusko** Polish patriot admired by English reformers

400 Surprised me even from a sleepless night;
And up I rose refreshed, and glad, and gay,
Resolving to begin that very day
These lines; and howsoever they be done,
I leave them as a father does his son.

1816   *1817*

Hymn to Pan

(from *Endymion*)

"O THOU, whose mighty palace roof doth hang
From jaggèd trunks, and overshadoweth
Eternal whispers, glooms, the birth, life, death
Of unseen flowers in heavy peacefulness;
Who lov'st to see the hamadryads dress
Their ruffled locks where meeting hazels darken;
And through whole solemn hours dost sit, and hearken
The dreary melody of bedded reeds—
In desolate places, where dank moisture breeds
10 The pipy hemlock to strange overgrowth;
Bethinking thee, how melancholy loth
Thou wast to lose fair Syrinx—do thou now,
By thy love's milky brow!
By all the trembling mazes that she ran,
Hear us, great Pan!

"O thou, for whose soul-soothing quiet, turtles
Passion their voices cooingly 'mong myrtles,
What time thou wanderest at eventide
Through sunny meadows, that outskirt the side
20 Of thine enmossèd realms: O thou, to whom
Broad leavèd fig trees even now foredoom
Their ripened fruitage; yellow girted bees
Their golden honeycombs; our village leas

1 **O thou** etc. from book I of *Endymion*. The hymn is sung by a chorus of Latmian shepherds during a festival in honour of Pan, god of forests and pastures 5 **hamadryads** tree nymphs 12 **Syrinx** nymph loved by Pan 16 **turtles** turtledoves

Their fairest blossomed beans and poppied corn;
The chuckling linnet its five young unborn,
To sing for thee; low creeping strawberries
Their summer coolness; pent up butterflies
Their freckled wings; yea, the fresh budding year
All its completions—be quickly near,
By every wind that nods the mountain pine,   30
O forester divine!

"Thou, to whom every faun and satyr flies
For willing service; whether to surprise
The squatted hare while in half sleeping fit;
Or upward ragged precipices flit
To save poor lambkins from the eagle's maw;
Or by mysterious enticement draw
Bewildered shepherds to their path again;
Or to tread breathless round the frothy main,
And gather up all fancifullest shells   40
For thee to tumble into Naiads' cells,
And, being hidden, laugh at their out-peeping;
Or to delight thee with fantastic leaping,
The while they pelt each other on the crown
With silvery oak apples, and fir cones brown—
By all the echoes that about thee ring,
Hear us, O satyr king!

"O Hearkener to the loud clapping shears,
While ever and anon to his shorn peers
A ram goes bleating: Winder of the horn,   50
When snouted wild-boars routing tender corn
Anger our huntsmen: Breather round our farms,
To keep off mildews, and all weather harms:
Strange ministrant of undescribèd sounds,
That come a swooning over hollow grounds,
And wither drearily on barren moors:
Dread opener of the mysterious doors
Leading to universal knowledge—see,
Great son of Dryope,
The many that are come to pay their vows   60
With leaves about their brows!

41 **Naiad** water nymph   51 **routing** tearing up

"Be still the unimaginable lodge
For solitary thinkings; such as dodge
Conception to the very bourne of heaven,
Then leave the naked brain: be still the leaven,
That spreading in this dull and clodded earth
Gives it a touch ethereal—a new birth:
Be still a symbol of immensity;
A firmament reflected in a sea;
70   An element filling the space between;
An unknown—but no more: we humbly screen
With uplift hands our foreheads, lowly bending,
And giving out a shout most heaven rending,
Conjure thee to receive our humble Pæan,
Upon thy Mount Lycean!"

1817   *1818*

Stanzas

In a drear-nighted December,
    Too happy, happy tree,
Thy branches ne'er remember
    Their green felicity:
    The north cannot undo them,
    With a sleety whistle through them;
    Nor frozen thawings glue them
        From budding at the prime.

In a drear-nighted December,
10   Too happy, happy brook,
Thy bubblings ne'er remember
    Apollo's summer look;
    But with a sweet forgetting,
    They stay their crystal fretting,
    Never, never petting
        About the frozen time.

Ah! would 'twere so with many
    A gentle girl and boy!

74 **Paean** song of thanksgiving 75 **Lycean** of Lyceus, a mountain
in Arcadia, sacred to Pan 15 **petting** sulking

But were there ever any
    Writhed not at passèd joy?   20
To know the change and feel it,
When there is none to heal it,
Nor numbèd sense to steel it,
    Was never said in rhyme.

1817   *1829*

Lines on the Mermaid Tavern

Souls of Poets dead and gone,
What Elysium have ye known,
Happy field or mossy cavern,
Choicer than the Mermaid Tavern?
Have ye tippled drink more fine
Than mine host's Canary wine?
Or are fruits of Paradise
Sweeter than those dainty pies
Of venison? O generous food!
Drest as though bold Robin Hood   10
Would, with his maid Marian,
Sup and bowse from horn and can.

    I have heard that on a day
Mine host's sign-board flew away,
Nobody knew whither, till
An astrologer's old quill
To a sheepskin gave the story,
Said he saw you in your glory,
Underneath a new old sign
Sipping beverage divine,   20
And pledging with contented smack
The Mermaid in the Zodiac.

    Souls of Poets dead and gone,
What Elysium have ye known,

4 Mermaid Tavern traditionally associated with Elizabethan poets
such as Shakespeare and Ben Jonson **12 bowse** drink or booze

Happy field or mossy cavern,
Choicer than the Mermaid Tavern?

1818   *1820*

Song

The stranger lighted from his steed,
    And ere he spake a word,
He seized my lady's lily hand,
    And kissed it all unheard.

The stranger walked into the hall,
    And ere he spake a word,
He kissed my lady's cherry lips,
    And kissed 'em all unheard.

The stranger walked into the bower,—
    But my lady first did go,—
Aye hand in hand into the bower,
    Where my lord's roses blow.

My lady's maid had a silken scarf,
    And a golden ring had she,
And a kiss from the stranger, as off he went
    Again on his fair palfrey.

1818   *1820*

Isabella

OR, THE POT OF BASIL

FAIR Isabel, poor simple Isabel!
    Lorenzo, a young palmer in Love's eye!
They could not in the self-same mansion dwell
    Without some stir of heart, some malady;
They could not sit at meals but feel how well
    It soothèd each to be the other by;

2 **palmer** pilgrim

They could not, sure, beneath the same roof sleep
But to each other dream, and nightly weep.

With every morn their love grew tenderer,
 With every eve deeper and tenderer still;   **10**
He might not in house, field, or garden stir,
 But her full shape would all his seeing fill;
And his continual voice was pleasanter
 To her, than noise of trees or hidden rill;
Her lute-string gave an echo of his name,
She spoilt her half-done broidery with the same.

He knew whose gentle hand was at the latch,
 Before the door had given her to his eyes;
And from her chamber-window he would catch
 Her beauty farther than the falcon spies;   **20**
And constant as her vespers would he watch,
 Because her face was turned to the same skies;
And with sick longing all the night outwear,
To hear her morning-step upon the stair.

A whole long month of May in this sad plight
 Made their cheeks paler by the break of June:
"To-morrow will I bow to my delight,
 To-morrow will I ask my lady's boon."—
"O may I never see another night,
 Lorenzo, if thy lips breathe not love's tune."— **30**
So spake they to their pillows; but, alas,
Honeyless days and days did he let pass;

Until sweet Isabella's untouched cheek
 Fell sick within the rose's just domain,
Fell thin as a young mother's, who doth seek
 By every lull to cool her infant's pain:
"How ill she is," said he, "I may not speak,
 And yet I will, and tell my love all plain:
If looks speak love-laws, I will drink her tears,
And at the least 'twill startle off her cares."   **40**

So said he one fair morning, and all day
 His heart beat awfully against his side;

42 **awfully** with a feeling of awe

And to his heart he inwardly did pray
    For power to speak; but still the ruddy tide
Stifled his voice, and pulsed resolve away—
    Fevered his high conceit of such a bride,
Yet brought him to the meekness of a child:
Alas! when passion is both meek and wild!

So once more he had waked and anguishèd
50   A dreary night of love and misery,
If Isabel's quick eye had not been wed
    To every symbol on his forehead high;
She saw it waxing very pale and dead,
    And straight all flushed; so, lispèd tenderly,
"Lorenzo!"—here she ceased her timid quest,
But in her tone and look he read the rest.

"O Isabella, I can half perceive
    That I may speak my grief into thine ear;
If thou didst ever anything believe,
60   Believe how I love thee, believe how near
My soul is to its doom: I would not grieve
    Thy hand by unwelcome pressing, would not fear
Thine eyes by gazing; but I cannot live
Another night, and not my passion shrive.

"Love! thou are leading me from wintry cold,
    Lady! thou leadest me to summer clime,
And I must taste the blossoms that unfold
    In its ripe warmth this gracious morning time."
So said, his erewhile timid lips grew bold,
70   And poesied with hers in dewy rhyme:
Great bliss was with them, and great happiness
Grew, like a lusty flower in June's caress.

Parting they seemed to tread upon the air,
    Twin roses by the zephyr blown apart
Only to meet again more close, and share
    The inward fragrance of each other's heart.
She, to her chamber gone, a ditty fair
    Sang, of delicious love and honeyed dart;

46 **conceit** opinion

He with light steps went up a western hill,
And bade the sun farewell, and joyed his fill.   80

All close they met again, before the dusk
   Had taken from the stars its pleasant veil,
All close they met, all eves, before the dusk
   Had taken from the stars its pleasant veil,
Close in a bower of hyacinth and musk,
   Unknown of any, free from whispering tale.
Ah! better had it been for ever so,
Than idle ears should pleasure in their woe.

Were they unhappy then?—It cannot be—
   Too many tears for lovers have been shed,   90
Too many sighs give we to them in fee,
   Too much of pity after they are dead,
Too many doleful stories do we see,
   Whose matter in bright gold were best be read;
Except in such a page where Theseus' spouse
Over the pathless waves towards him bows.

But, for the general award of love,
   The little sweet doth kill much bitterness;
Though Dido silent is in under-grove,
   And Isabella's was a great distress,   100
Though young Lorenzo in warm Indian clove
   Was not embalmed, this truth is not the less
Even bees, the little almsmen of spring-bowers,
Know there is richest juice in poison-flowers.

With her two brothers this fair lady dwelt,
   Enrichèd from ancestral merchandize,
And for them many a weary hand did swelt
   In torchèd mines and noisy factories,
And many once proud-quivered loins did melt
   In blood from stinging whip;—with hollow eyes   110
Many all day in dazzling river stood,
To take the rich-ored driftings of the flood.

91 **in fee** as their rightful possession 95 **Theseus' spouse** Ariadne
109 **proud-quivered** which once proudly bore quivers when hunting

For them the Ceylon diver held his breath,
  And went all naked to the hungry shark;
For them his ears gushed blood; for them in death
  The seal on the cold ice with piteous bark
Lay full of darts; for them alone did seethe
  A thousand men in troubles wide and dark:
Half-ignorant, they turned an easy wheel,
120 That set sharp racks at work, to pinch and peel.

Why were they proud? Because their marble founts
  Gushed with more pride than do a wretch's tears?—
Why were they proud? Because fair orange-mounts
  Were of more soft ascent than lazar stairs?—
Why were they proud? Because red-lined accounts
  Were richer than the songs of Grecian years?—
Why were they proud? again we ask aloud,
Why in the name of Glory were they proud?

Yet were these Florentines as self-retired
130 In hungry pride and gainful cowardice,
As two close Hebrews in that land inspired,
  Paled in and vineyarded from beggar-spies;
The hawks of ship-mast forests—the untired
  And panniered mules for ducats and old lies—
Quick cat's-paws on the generous stray-away,—
Great wits in Spanish, Tuscan, and Malay.

How was it these same ledger-men could spy
  Fair Isabella in her downy nest?
How could they find out in Lorenzo's eye
140 A straying from his toil? Hot Egypt's pest
Into their vision covetous and sly!
  How could these money-bags see east and west?—
Yet so they did—and every dealer fair
Must see behind, as doth the hunted hare.

O eloquent and famed Boccaccio!
  Of thee we now should ask forgiving boon,

119 **they** the brothers 124 **lazar** leper 132 **Paled** fenced 135 **Quick cat's-paws** quick to pounce on unsuspecting strangers 140 **Hot Egypt's pest** various kinds of pestilence inflicted on the Egyptians at the time of Moses 145 **Boccaccio** (1313-75) Italian author of the collection of prose stories called the *Decameron*. One of these stories provided the plot for Keats' poem.

And of thy spicy myrtles as they blow,
   And of thy roses amorous of the moon,
And of thy lillies, that do paler grow
   Now they can no more hear thy ghittern's tune,   150
For venturing syllables that ill beseem
The quiet glooms of such a piteous theme.

Grant thou a pardon here, and then the tale
   Shall move on soberly, as it is meet;
There is no other crime, no mad assail
   To make old prose in modern rhyme more sweet:
But it is done—succeed the verse or fail—
   To honour thee, and thy gone spirit greet;
To stead thee as a verse in English tongue,
An echo of thee in the north-wind sung.   160

These brethren having found by many signs
   What love Lorenzo for their sister had,
And how she loved him too, each unconfines
   His bitter thoughts to other, well nigh mad
That he, the servant of their trade designs,
   Should in their sister's love be blithe and glad,
When 'twas their plan to coax her by degrees
To some high noble and his olive-trees.

And many a jealous conference had they,
   And many times they bit their lips alone,   170
Before they fixed upon a surest way
   To make the youngster for his crime atone;
And at the last, these men of cruel clay
   Cut Mercy with a sharp knife to the bone;
For they resolvèd in some forest dim
To kill Lorenzo, and there bury him.

So on a pleasant morning, as he leant
   Into the sun-rise, o'er the balustrade
Of the garden-terrace, towards him they bent
   Their footing through the dews; and to him said,   180
"You seem there in the quiet of content,
   Lorenzo, and we are most loth to invade

150 **ghittern** guitar   159 **stead** establish

Calm speculation; but if you are wise,
Bestride your steed while cold is in the skies.

"To-day we purpose, ay, this hour we mount
 To spur three leagues towards the Apennine;
Come down, we pray thee, ere the hot sun count
 His dewy rosary on the eglantine."
Lorenzo, courteously as he was wont,
190 Bowed a fair greeting to these serpents' whine;
And went in haste, to get in readiness,
With belt, and spur, and bracing huntsman's dress.

And as he to the court-yard passed along,
 Each third step did he pause, and listened oft
If he could hear his lady's matin-song,
 Or the light whisper of her footstep soft;
And as he thus over his passion hung,
 He heard a laugh full musical aloft;
When, looking up, he saw her features bright
200 Smile through an in-door lattice, all delight.

"Love, Isabel!" said he, "I was in pain
 Lest I should miss to bid thee a good morrow:
Ah! what if I should lose thee, when so fain
 I am to stifle all the heavy sorrow
Of a poor three hours' absence? but we'll gain
 Out of the amorous dark what day doth borrow.
Good bye! I'll soon be back."—"Good bye!" said she:—
And as he went she chanted merrily.

So the two brothers and their murdered man
210 Rode past fair Florence, to where Arno's stream
Gurgles through straitened banks, and still doth fan
 Itself with dancing bulrush, and the bream
Keeps head against the freshets. Sick and wan
 The brothers' faces in the ford did seem,
Lorenzo's flush with love.—They passed the water
Into a forest quiet for the slaughter.

There was Lorenzo slain and buried in,
 There in that forest did his great love cease;

Ah! when a soul doth thus its freedom win,
   It aches in loneliness—is ill at peace   220
As the break-covert blood-hounds of such sin:
   They dipped their swords in the water, and did tease
Their horses homeward, with convulsèd spur,
Each richer by his being a murderer.

They told their sister how, with sudden speed,
   Lorenzo had ta'en ship for foreign lands,
Because of some great urgency and need
   In their affairs, requiring trusty hands.
Poor Girl! put on thy stifling widow's weed,
   And 'scape at once from Hope's accursèd bands;   230
To-day thou wilt not see him, nor to-morrow,
And the next day will be a day of sorrow.

She weeps alone for pleasures not to be;
   Sorely she wept until the night came on,
And then, instead of love, O misery!
   She brooded o'er the luxury alone:
His image in the dusk she seemed to see,
   And to the silence made a gentle moan,
Spreading her perfect arms upon the air,
And on her couch low murmuring "Where? O where?"   240

But Selfishness, Love's cousin, held not long
   Its fiery vigil in her single breast;
She fretted for the golden hour, and hung
   Upon the time with feverish unrest—
Not long—for soon into her heart a throng
   Of higher occupants, a richer zest,
Came tragic; passion not to be subdued,
And sorrow for her love in travels rude.

In the mid days of autumn, on their eves
   The breath of Winter comes from far away,   250
And the sick west continually bereaves
   Of some gold tinge, and plays a roundelay
Of death among the bushes and the leaves
   To make all bare before he dares to stray

221 **break-covert** exposed by coming out from a place of con-
cealment

From his north cavern. So sweet Isabel
By gradual decay from beauty fell,

Because Lorenzo came not. Oftentimes
　　She asked her brothers, with an eye all pale,
Striving to be itself, what dungeon climes
260　Could keep him off so long? They spake a tale
Time after time, to quiet her. Their crimes
　　Came on them, like a smoke from Hinnom's vale;
And every night in dreams they groaned aloud,
To see their sister in her snowy shroud.

And she had died in drowsy ignorance,
　　But for a thing more deadly dark than all;
It came like a fierce potion, drunk by chance,
　　Which saves a sick man from the feathered pall
For some few gasping moments; like a lance,
270　Waking an Indian from his cloudy hall
With cruel pierce, and bringing him again
Sense of the gnawing fire at heart and brain.

It was a vision.—In the drowsy gloom,
　　The dull of midnight, at her couch's foot
Lorenzo stood, and wept: the forest tomb
　　Had marred his glossy hair which once could shoot
Lustre into the sun, and put cold doom
　　Upon his lips, and taken the soft lute
From his lorn voice, and past his loamèd ears
280 Had made a miry channel for his tears.

Strange sound it was, when the pale shadow spake;
　　For there was striving, in its piteous tongue,
To speak as when on earth it was awake,
　　And Isabella on its music hung:
Languor there was in it, and tremulous shake,
　　As in a palsied Druid's harp unstrung;
And through it moaned a ghostly under-song,
Like hoarse night-gusts sepulchral briars among.

Its eyes, though wild, were still all dewy bright
290　With love, and kept all phantom fear aloof

262 **Hinnom's vale** valley south of Jerusalem where dead bodies
were burned 268 **pall** cloth covering a coffin

From the poor girl by magic of their light,
  The while it did unthread the horrid woof
Of the late darkened time,—the murderous spite
  Of pride and avarice,—the dark pine roof
In the forest,—and the sodden turfèd dell,
Where, without any word, from stabs he fell.

Saying moreover, "Isabel, my sweet!
  Red whortle-berries droop above my head,
And a large flint-stone weighs upon my feet;
  Around me beeches and high chestnuts shed   300
Their leaves and prickly nuts; a sheep-fold bleat
  Comes from beyond the river to my bed:
Go, shed one tear upon my heather-bloom,
And it shall comfort me within the tomb.

"I am a shadow now, alas! alas!
  Upon the skirts of human-nature dwelling
Alone: I chant alone the holy mass,
  While little sounds of life are round me knelling,
And glossy bees at noon do fieldward pass,
  And many a chapel bell the hour is telling,   310
Paining me through: those sounds grow strange **to me**,
And thou art distant in Humanity.

"I know what was, I feel full well what is,
  And I should rage, if spirits could go mad;
Though I forget the taste of earthly bliss,
  That paleness warms my grave, as though I had
A Seraph chosen from the bright abyss
  To be my spouse: thy paleness makes me glad;
Thy beauty grows upon me, and I feel
A greater love through all my essence steal."   320

The Spirit mourned "Adieu!"—dissolved and left
  The atom darkness in a slow turmoil;
As when of healthful midnight sleep bereft,
  Thinking on rugged hours and fruitless toil,
We put our eyes into a pillowy cleft,
  And see the spangly gloom froth up and boil:
It made sad Isabella's eyelids ache,
And in the dawn she started up awake;

"Ha! ha!" said she, "I knew not this hard life,
330   I thought the worst was simple misery;
I thought some Fate with pleasure or with strife
    Portioned us—happy days, or else to die;
But there is crime—a brother's bloody knife!
    Sweet Spirit, thou hast schooled my infancy:
I'll visit thee for this, and kiss thine eyes,
And greet thee morn and even in the skies."

When the full morning came, she had devised
    How she might secret to the forest hie;
How she might find the clay, so dearly prized,
340   And sing to it one latest lullaby;
How her short absence might be unsurmised,
    While she the inmost of the dream would try.
Resolved, she took with her an agèd nurse,
And went into that dismal forest-hearse.

See, as they creep along the river side,
    How she doth whisper to that agèd Dame,
And, after looking round the champaign wide,
    Shows her a knife.—"What feverous hectic flame
Burns in thee, child?—What good can thee betide,
350   That thou should'st smile again?"—The evening came,
And they had found Lorenzo's earthy bed;
The flint was there, the berries at his head.

Who hath not loitered in a green church-yard,
    And let his spirit, like a demon-mole,
Work through the clayey soil and gravel hard,
    To see scull, coffined bones, and funeral stole;
Pitying each form that hungry Death hath marred,
    And filling it once more with human soul?
Ah! this is holiday to what was felt
360 When Isabella by Lorenzo knelt.

She gazed into the fresh-thrown mould, as though
    One glance did fully all its secrets tell;
Clearly she saw, as other eyes would know
    Pale limbs at bottom of a crystal well;
Upon the murderous spot she seemed to grow,
    Like to a native lilly of the dell:

Then with her knife, all sudden, she began
To dig more fervently than misers can.

Soon she turned up a soilèd glove, whereon
    Her silk had played in purple phantasies,   370
She kissed it with a lip more chill than stone,
    And put it in her bosom, where it dries
And freezes utterly unto the bone
    Those dainties made to still an infant's cries:
Then 'gan she work again; nor stayed her care,
But to throw back at times her veiling hair.

That old nurse stood beside her wondering,
    Until her heart felt pity to the core
At sight of such a dismal labouring,
    And so she kneelèd, with her locks all hoar,   380
And put her lean hands to the horrid thing:
    Three hours they laboured at this travail sore;
At last they felt the kernel of the grave,
And Isabella did not stamp and rave.

Ah! wherefore all this wormy· circumstance?
    Why linger at the yawning tomb so long?
O for the gentleness of old Romance,
    The simple plaining of a minstrel's song!
Fair reader, at the old tale take a glance,
    For here, in truth, it doth not well belong   390
To speak:—O turn thee to the very tale,
And taste the music of that vision pale.

With duller steel than the Persèan sword
    They cut away no formless monster's head,
But one, whose gentleness did well accord
    With death, as life. The ancient harps have said,
Love never dies, but lives, immortal Lord:
    If Love impersonate was ever dead,
Pale Isabella kissed it, and low moaned.
'Twas love; cold,—dead indeed, but not dethroned.   400

In anxious secrecy they took it home,
    And then the prize was all for Isabel:

393 **Persean** of Perseus, who cut off the head of the monster,
Medusa

She calmed its wild hair with a golden comb,
　　And all around each eye's sepulchral cell
Pointed each fringèd lash; the smearèd loam
　　With tears, as chilly as a dripping well,
She drenched away:—and still she combed, and kept
Sighing all day—and still she kissed, and wept.

Then in a silken scarf,—sweet with the dews
410　　Of precious flowers plucked in Araby,
And divine liquids come with odorous ooze
　　Through the cold serpent-pipe refreshfully,—
She wrapped it up; and for its tomb did choose
　　A garden-pot, wherein she laid it by,
And covered it with mould, and o'er it set
Sweet Basil, which her tears kept ever wet.

And she forgot the stars, the moon, and sun,
　　And she forgot the blue above the trees,
And she forgot the dells where waters run,
420　　And she forgot the chilly autumn breeze;
She had no knowledge when the day was done,
　　And the new morn she saw not: but in peace
Hung over her sweet Basil evermore,
And moistened it with tears unto the core.

And so she ever fed it with thin tears,
　　Whence thick, and green, and beautiful it grew,
So that it smelt more balmy than its peers
　　Of Basil-tufts in Florence; for it drew
Nurture besides, and life, from human fears,
430　　From the fast mouldering head there shut from view:
So that the jewel, safely casketed,
Came forth, and in perfumèd leafits spread.

O Melancholy, linger here awhile!
　　O Music, Music, breathe despondingly!
O Echo, Echo, from some sombre isle,
　　Unknown, Lethean, sigh to us—O sigh!
Spirits in grief, lift up your heads, and smile;
　　Lift up your heads, sweet Spirits, heavily,
And make a pale light in your cypress glooms,
440 Tinting with silver wan your marble tombs.

Moan hither, all ye syllables of woe,
    From the deep throat of sad Melpomene!
Through bronzèd lyre in tragic order go,
    And touch the strings into a mystery;
Sound mournfully upon the winds and low;
    For simple Isabel is soon to be
Among the dead: She withers, like a palm
Cut by an Indian for its juicy balm.

O leave the palm to wither by itself;
    Let not quick Winter chill its dying hour!—   450
It may not be—those Baälites of pelf,
    Her brethren, noted the continual shower
From her dead eyes; and many a curious elf,
    Among her kindred, wondered that such dower
Of youth and beauty should be thrown aside
By one marked out to be a Noble's bride.

And, furthermore, her brethren wondered much
    Why she sat drooping by the Basil green,
And why it flourished, as by magic touch;
    Greatly they wondered what the thing might mean: 460
They could not surely give belief, that such
    A very nothing would have power to wean
Her from her own fair youth, and pleasures gay,
And even remembrance of her love's delay.

Therefore they watched a time when they might sift
    This hidden whim; and long they watched in vain;
For seldom did she go to chapel-shrift,
    And seldom felt she any hunger-pain;
And when she left, she hurried back, as swift
    As bird on wing to breast its eggs again;   470
And, patient as a hen-bird, sat her there
Beside her Basil, weeping through her hair.

Yet they contrived to steal the Basil-pot,
    And to examine it in secret place:
The thing was vile with green and livid spot,
    And yet they knew it was Lorenzo's face:

442 **Melpomene** muse of tragedy 451 **Baälites** worshippers of
gold

The guerdon of their murder they had got,
 And so left Florence in a moment's space,
Never to turn again.—Away they went,
480 With blood upon their heads, to banishment.

O Melancholy, turn thine eyes away!
 O Music, Music, breathe despondingly!
O Echo, Echo, on some other day,
 From isles Lethean, sigh to us—O sigh!
Spirits of grief, sing not your "Well-a-way!"
 For Isabel, sweet Isabel, will die;
Will die a death too lone and incomplete,
Now they have ta'en away her Basil sweet.

Piteous she looked on dead and senseless things,
490 Asking for her lost Basil amorously;
And with melodious chuckle in the strings
 Of her lorn voice, she oftentimes would cry
After the Pilgrim in his wanderings,
 To ask him where her Basil was; and why
'Twas hid from her: "For cruel 'tis," said she,
"To steal my Basil-pot away from me."

And so she pined, and so she died forlorn,
 Imploring for her Basil to the last.
No heart was there in Florence but did mourn
500 In pity of her love, so overcast.
And a sad ditty of this story born
 From mouth to mouth through all the country passed:
Still is the burthen sung—"O cruelty,
To steal my Basil-pot away from me!"

1818   *1820*

Lines Written in the Highlands After a Visit to Burns's Country

THERE is a charm in footing slow across a silent plain,
Where patriot battle has been fought, where glory had the
  gain;
There is a pleasure on the heath where Druids old have
  been,
Where mantles grey have rustled by and swept the nettles
  green;
There is a joy in every spot made known by times of old,
New to the feet, although each tale a hundred times be told;
There is a deeper joy than all, more solemn in the heart,
More parching to the tongue than all, of more divine a smart,
When weary steps forget themselves upon a pleasant turf,
Upon hot sand, or flinty road, or sea-shore iron scurf,   10
Toward the castle or the cot, where long ago was born
One who was great through mortal days, and died of fame
  unshorn,
Light heather-bells may tremble then, but they are far away;
Wood-lark may sing from sandy fern,—the Sun may hear
  his lay;
Runnels may kiss the grass on shelves and shallows clear,
But their low voices are not heard, though come on travels
  drear;
Blood-red the Sun may set behind black mountain peaks;
Blue tides may sluice and drench their time in caves and
  weedy creeks;
Eagles may seem to sleep wing-wide upon the air;
Ring-doves may fly convulsed across to some high-cedared
  lair;   20
But the forgotten eye is still fast lidded to the ground,
As Palmer's, that with weariness, mid-desert shrine hath
  found.
At such a time the soul's a child, in childhood is the brain;

10 **scurf** scaly surface 12 **One** Burns. Keats admired his poetry
but was so appalled to think of the "miserable" kind of life Burns
had led in Scotland that it was like a painful nightmare for him to
visit Burns' cottage. See Keats' letters of July, 1818.

Forgotten is the worldly heart—alone, it beats in vain.—
Aye, if a madman could have leave to pass a healthful day
To tell his forehead's swoon and faint when first began de-
        cay,
He might make tremble many a one whose spirit had gone
        forth
To find a Bard's low cradle-place about the silent North!
Scanty the hour and few the steps beyond the bourn of care,
30 Beyond the sweet and bitter world,—beyond it unaware!
Scanty the hour and few the steps, because a longer stay
Would bar return, and make a man forget his mortal way:
O horrible! to lose the sight of well remembered face,
Of Brother's eyes, of Sister's brow—constant to every place;
Filling the air, as on we move, with portraiture intense;
More warm than those heroic tints that pain a painter's
        sense,
When shapes of old come striding by, and visages of old,
Locks shining black, hair scanty grey, and passions mani-
        fold.
No, no, that horror cannot be, for at the cable's length
Man feels the gentle anchor pull and gladdens in its
40   strength:—
One hour, half-idiot, he stands by mossy waterfall,
But in the very next he reads his soul's memorial:—
He reads it on the mountain's height, where chance he may
        sit down
Upon rough marble diadem—that hill's eternal crown.
Yet be his anchor e'er so fast, room is there for a prayer
That man may never lose his mind on mountains black and
        bare;
That he may stray league after league some great birth-
        place to find
And keep his vision clear from speck, his inward sight un-
        blind.

1818   *1822*

26 **forehead's swoon** how he became insane 29 **bourn** borderline
of sanity 34 **Brother's . . . brow** Keats was deeply distressed by
the recent departure of his brother and sister-in-law to America
39 **horror** madness and suicide 40 **anchor** probably his love for
his brother and sister-in-law, his "inducements to Life" as he calls
them in a letter of July 11, 1818 42 **memorial** history

Fancy

EVER let the fancy roam,
Pleasure never is at home:
At a touch sweet Pleasure melteth,
Like to bubbles when rain pelteth;
Then let wingèd Fancy wander
Through the thought still spread beyond her:
Open wide the mind's cage-door,
She'll dart forth, and cloudward soar.
O sweet Fancy! let her loose;
Summer's joys are spoilt by use,   10
And the enjoying of the Spring
Fades as does its blossoming;
Autumn's red-lipped fruitage too,
Blushing through the mist and dew,
Cloys with tasting: What do then?
Sit thee by the ingle, when
The sear faggot blazes bright,
Spirit of a winter's night;
When the soundless earth is muffled,
And the cakèd snow is shuffled   20
From the ploughboy's heavy shoon;
When the Night doth meet the Noon
In a dark conspiracy
To banish Even from her sky.
Sit thee there, and send abroad,
With a mind self-overawed,
Fancy, high-commissioned:—send her!
She has vassals to attend her:
She will bring, in spite of frost,
Beauties that the earth hath lost;   30
She will bring thee, all together,
All delights of summer weather;
All the buds and bells of May,
From dewy sward or thorny spray;
All the heapèd Autumn's wealth,
With a still, mysterious stealth:
She will mix these pleasures up
Like three fit wines in a cup,
And thou shalt quaff it:—thou shalt hear

40 Distant harvest-carols clear;
Rustle of the reapèd corn;
Sweet birds antheming the morn:
And, in the same moment—hark!
'Tis the early April lark,
Or the rooks, with busy caw,
Foraging for sticks and straw.
Thou shalt, at one glance, behold
The daisy and the marigold;
White-plumed lillies, and the first
50 Hedge-grown primrose that hath burst;
Shaded hyacinth, alway
Sapphire queen of the mid-May;
And every leaf, and every flower
Pearlèd with the self-same shower.
Thou shalt see the field-mouse peep
Meagre from its cellèd sleep;
And the snake all winter-thin
Cast on sunny bank its skin;
Freckled nest-eggs thou shalt see
60 Hatching in the hawthorn-tree,
When the hen-bird's wing doth rest
Quiet on her mossy nest;
Then the hurry and alarm
When the bee-hive casts its swarm;
Acorns ripe down-pattering,
While the autumn breezes sing.

Oh, sweet Fancy! let her loose;
Every thing is spoilt by use:
Where's the cheek that doth not fade,
70 Too much gazed at? Where's the maid
Whose lip mature is ever new?
Where's the eye, however blue,
Doth not weary? Where's the face
One would meet in every place?
Where's the voice, however soft,
One would hear so very oft?
At a touch sweet Pleasure melteth
Like to bubbles when rain pelteth.
Let, then, wingèd Fancy find

Thee a mistress to thy mind: 80
Dulcet-eyed as Ceres' daughter,
Ere the God of Torment taught her
How to frown and how to chide;
With a waist and with a side
White as Hebe's, when her zone
Slipt its golden clasp, and down
Fell her kirtle to her feet,
While she held the goblet sweet,
And Jove grew languid.—Break the mesh
Of the Fancy's silken leash;   90
Quickly break her prison-string
And such joys as these she'll bring.—
Let the wingèd Fancy roam,
Pleasure never is at home.

1818   *1820*

Ode

**WRITTEN ON THE BLANK PAGE BEFORE BEAUMONT AND
FLETCHER'S TRAGI-COMEDY "THE FAIR MAID OF THE INN"**

BARDS of Passion and of Mirth,
Ye have left your souls on earth!
Have ye souls in heaven too,
Double-lived in regions new?
Yes, and those of heaven commune
With the spheres of sun and moon;
With the noise of fountains wond'rous,
And the parle of voices thund'rous;
With the whisper of heaven's trees
And one another, in soft ease   10
Seated on Elysian lawns
Browsed by none but Dian's fawns
Underneath large blue-bells tented,
Where the daisies are rose-scented,

81 **daughter** Proserpine, carried off to the lower world by Pluto
85 **Hebe** Jove's cupbearer

And the rose herself has got
Perfume which on earth is not;
Where the nightingale doth sing
Not a senseless, trancèd thing,
But divine melodious truth;
20 Philosophic numbers smooth;
Tales and golden histories
Of heaven and its mysteries.

Thus ye live on high, and then
On the earth ye live again;
And the souls ye left behind you
Teach us, here, the way to find you,
Where your other souls are joying,
Never slumbered, never cloying.
Here, your earth-born souls still speak
30 To mortals, of their little week;
Of their sorrows and delights;
Of their passions and their spites;
Of their glory and their shame;
What doth strengthen and what maim.
Thus ye teach us, every day,
Wisdom, though fled far away.

Bards of Passion and of Mirth,
Ye have left your souls on earth!
Ye have souls in heaven too,
40 Double-lived in regions new!

1818 *1820*

Hyperion

A FRAGMENT

BOOK I

DEEP in the shady sadness of a vale
Far sunken from the healthy breath of morn,
Far from the fiery noon, and eve's one star,
Sat gray-haired Saturn, quiet as a stone,
Still as the silence round about his lair;
Forest on forest hung above his head
Like cloud on cloud. No stir of air was there,
Not so much life as on a summer's day
Robs not one light seed from the feathered grass,
But where the dead leaf fell, there did it rest.   10
A stream went voiceless by, still deadened more
By reason of his fallen divinity
Spreading a shade: the Naiad 'mid her reeds
Pressed her cold finger closer to her lips.

Along the margin-sand large foot-marks went,
No further than to where his feet had strayed,
And slept there since. Upon the sodden ground
His old right hand lay nerveless, listless, dead,
Unsceptred; and his realmless eyes were closed;
While his bowed head seemed list'ning to the Earth,   20
His ancient mother, for some comfort yet.

It seemed no force could wake him from his place;
But there came one, who with a kindred hand

4 **Saturn** king of the early race of gods known as Titans, was overthrown by his son, Jupiter, leader of the Olympians. As the poem opens, all but one of the Titan gods have been banished to the underworld. Hyperion, god of the sun, is the only Titan not yet overthrown, and his position is threatened by Apollo, the Olympian who will presumably succeed him. This story of the old order being replaced by the new is considerably modified by Keats. Instead of the Titans being shown as merely brutal, they are pictured as magnificent even in the bewilderment of defeat, yet lacking in certain other qualities possessed by the Olympians. 13 **Naiad** water nymph 23 **one** Hyperion's wife, Thea

Touched his wide shoulders, after bending low
With reverence, though to one who knew it not.
She was a Goddess of the infant world;
By her in stature the tall Amazon
Had stood a pigmy's height: she would have ta'en
Achilles by the hair and bent his neck;
30   Or with a finger stayed Ixion's wheel.
Her face was large as that of Memphian sphinx,
Pedestaled haply in a palace court,
When sages looked to Egypt for their lore.
But oh! how unlike marble was that face:
How beautiful, if sorrow had not made
Sorrow more beautiful than Beauty's self.
There was a listening fear in her regard,
As if calamity had but begun;
As if the vanward clouds of evil days
40   Had spent their malice, and the sullen rear
Was with its storèd thunder labouring up.
One hand she pressed upon that aching spot
Where beats the human heart, as if just there,
Though an immortal, she felt cruel pain:
The other upon Saturn's bended neck
She laid, and to the level of his ear
Leaning with parted lips, some words she spake
In solemn tenour and deep organ tone:
Some mourning words, which in our feeble tongue
50   Would come in these like accents; O how frail
To that large utterance of the early Gods!
"Saturn, look up!—though wherefore, poor old King?
I have no comfort for thee, no not one:
I cannot say, 'O wherefore sleepest thou?'
For heaven is parted from thee, and the earth
Knows thee not, thus afflicted, for a God;
And ocean too, with all its solemn noise,
Has from thy sceptre passed; and all the air
Is emptied of thine hoary majesty.
60   Thy thunder, conscious of the new command,
Rumbles reluctant o'er our fallen house;
And thy sharp lightning in unpractised hands
Scorches and burns our once serene domain.

30 **Ixion's wheel** perpetually turning wheel on which **Ixion was** punished

O aching time! O moments big as years!
All as ye pass swell out the monstrous truth,
And press it so upon our weary griefs
That unbelief has not a space to breathe.
Saturn, sleep on:—O thoughtless, why did I
Thus violate thy slumbrous solitude?
Why should I ope thy melancholy eyes?   70
Saturn, sleep on! while at thy feet I weep."

    As when, upon a trancèd summer-night,
Those green-robed senators of mighty woods,
Tall oaks, branch-charmèd by the earnest stars,
Dream, and so dream all night without a stir,
Save from one gradual solitary gust
Which comes upon the silence, and dies off,
As if the ebbing air had but one wave;
So came these words and went; the while in tears
She touched her fair large forehead to the ground,   80
Just where her fallen hair might be outspread
A soft and silken mat for Saturn's feet.
One moon, with alteration slow, had shed
Her silver seasons four upon the night,
And still these two were postured motionless,
Like natural sculpture in cathedral cavern;
The frozen God still couchant on the earth,
And the sad Goddess weeping at his feet:
Until at length old Saturn lifted up
His faded eyes, and saw his kingdom gone,   90
And all the gloom and sorrow of the place,
And that fair kneeling Goddess; and then spake,
As with a palsied tongue, and while his beard
Shook horrid with such aspen-malady:
"O tender spouse of gold Hyperion,
Thea, I feel thee ere I see thy face;
Look up, and let me see our doom in it;
Look up, and tell me if this feeble shape
Is Saturn's; tell me, if thou hear'st the voice
Of Saturn; tell me, if this wrinkling brow,   100
Naked and bare of its great diadem,
Peers like the front of Saturn. Who had power
To make me desolate? whence came the strength?
How was it nurtured to such bursting forth,

While Fate seemed strangled in my nervous grasp?
But it is so; and I am smothered up,
And buried from all godlike exercise
Of influence benign on planets pale,
Of admonitions to the winds and seas,
110 Of peaceful sway above man's harvesting,
And all those acts which Deity supreme
Doth ease its heart of love in.—I am gone
Away from my own bosom: I have left
My strong identity, my real self,
Somewhere between the throne, and where I sit
Here on this spot of earth. Search, Thea, search!
Open thine eyes eterne, and sphere them round
Upon all space: space starred, and lorn of light;
Space regioned with life-air; and barren void;
120 Spaces of fire, and all the yawn of hell.—
Search, Thea, search! and tell me, if thou seest
A certain shape or shadow, making way
With wings or chariot fierce to repossess
A heaven he lost erewhile: it must—it must
Be of ripe progress—Saturn must be King.
Yes, there must be a golden victory;
There must be Gods thrown down, and trumpets blown
Of triumph calm, and hymns of festival
Upon the gold clouds metropolitan,
130 Voices of soft proclaim, and silver stir
Of strings in hollow shells; and there shall be
Beautiful things made new, for the surprise
Of the sky-children; I will give command:
Thea! Thea! Thea! where is Saturn?"

This passion lifted him upon his feet,
And made his hands to struggle in the air,
His Druid locks to shake and ooze with sweat,
His eyes to fever out, his voice to cease.
He stood, and heard not Thea's sobbing deep;
140 A little time, and then again he snatched
Utterance thus.—"But cannot I create?
Cannot I form? Cannot I fashion forth
Another world, another universe,
To overbear and crumble this to nought?
Where is another Chaos? Where?"—That word

Found way unto Olympus, and made quake
The rebel three.—Thea was startled up,
And in her bearing was a sort of hope,
As thus she quick-voiced spake, yet full of awe.
"This cheers our fallen house: come to our friends,   150
O Saturn! come away, and give them heart;
I know the covert, for thence came I hither."
Thus brief; then with beseeching eyes she went
With backward footing through the shade a space:
He followed, and she turned to lead the way
Through agèd boughs, that yielded like the mist
Which eagles cleave upmounting from their nest.

    Meanwhile in other realms big tears were shed,
More sorrow like to this, and such like woe,
Too huge for mortal tongue or pen of scribe: 160
The Titans fierce, self-hid, or prison-bound,
Groaned for the old allegiance once more,
And listened in sharp pain for Saturn's voice.
But one of the whole mammoth-brood still kept
His sov'reignty, and rule, and majesty;—
Blazing Hyperion on his orbèd fire
Still sat, still snuffed the incense, teeming up
From Man to the sun's God; yet unsecure:
For as among us mortals omens drear
Fright and perplex, so also shuddered he—   170
Not at dog's howl, or gloom-bird's hated screech,
Or the familiar visiting of one
Upon the first toll of his passing-bell,
Or prophesyings of the midnight lamp;
But horrors, portioned to a giant nerve,
Oft made Hyperion ache. His palace bright
Bastioned with pyramids of glowing gold,
And touched with shade of bronzèd obelisks,
Glared a blood-red through all its thousand courts,
Arches, and domes, and fiery galleries;   180
And all its curtains of Aurorian clouds
Flushed angerly: while sometimes eagle's wings,
Unseen before by Gods or wondering men,
Darkened the place; and neighing steeds were heard,
Not heard before by Gods or wondering men.

147 **rebel three** Jupiter, Neptune, and Pluto

Also, when he would taste the spicy wreaths
Of incense, breathed aloft from sacred hills,
Instead of sweets, his ample palate took
Savour of poisonous brass and metal sick:
190 And so, when harboured in the sleepy west,
After the full completion of fair day,—
For rest divine upon exalted couch
And slumber in the arms of melody,
He paced away the pleasant hours of ease
With stride colossal, on from hall to hall;
While far within each aisle and deep recess,
His wingèd minions in close clusters stood,
Amazed and full of fear; like anxious men
Who on wide plains gather in panting troops,
200 When earthquakes jar their battlements and towers.
Even now, while Saturn, roused from icy trance,
Went step for step with Thea through the woods,
Hyperion, leaving twilight in the rear,
Came slope upon the threshold of the west;
Then, as was wont, his palace-door flew ope
In smoothest silence, save what solemn tubes,
Blown by the serious Zephyrs, gave of sweet
And wandering sounds, slow-breathèd melodies;
And like a rose in vermeil tint and shape,
210 In fragrance soft, and coolness to the eye,
That inlet to severe magnificence
Stood full blown, for the God to enter in.

He entered, but he entered full of wrath;
His flaming robes streamed out beyond his heels,
And gave a roar, as if of earthly fire,
That scared away the meek ethereal Hours
And made their dove-wings tremble. On he flared,
From stately nave to nave, from vault to vault,
Through bowers of fragrant and enwreathèd light,
220 And diamond-pavèd lustrous long arcades,
Until he reached the great main cupola;
There standing fierce beneath, he stamped his foot,
And from the basements deep to the high towers
Jarred his own golden region; and before
The quavering thunder thereupon had ceased,

206 **tubes** musical wind instruments

His voice leapt out, despite of godlike curb,
To this result: "O dreams of day and night!
O monstrous forms! O effigies of pain!
O spectres busy in a cold, cold gloom!
O lank-eared Phantoms of black-weeded pools! 230
Why do I know ye? why have I seen ye? why
Is my eternal essence thus distraught
To see and to behold these horrors new?
Saturn is fallen, am I too to fall?
Am I to leave this haven of my rest,
This cradle of my glory, this soft clime,
This calm luxuriance of blissful light,
These crystalline pavilions, and pure fanes,
Of all my lucent empire? It is left
Deserted, void, nor any haunt of mine. 240
The blaze, the splendor, and the symmetry,
I cannot see—but darkness, death and darkness.
Even here, into my centre of repose,
The shady visions come to domineer,
Insult, and blind, and stifle up my pomp.—
Fall! —No, by Tellus and her briny robes!
Over the fiery frontier of my realms
I will advance a terrible right arm
Shall scare that infant Thunderer, rebel Jove,
And bid old Saturn take his throne again."— 250
He spake, and ceased, the while a heavier threat
Held struggle with his throat but came not forth;
For as in theatres of crowded men
Hubbub increases more they call out "Hush!"
So at Hyperion's words the Phantoms pale
Bestirred themselves, thrice horrible and cold;
And from the mirrored level where he stood
A mist arose, as from a scummy marsh.
At this, through all his bulk an agony
Crept gradual, from the feet unto the crown, 260
Like a lithe serpent vast and muscular
Making slow way, with head and neck convulsed
From over-strainèd might. Released, he fled
To the eastern gates, and full six dewy hours
Before the dawn in season due should blush,
He breathed fierce breath against the sleepy portals,
Cleared them of heavy vapours, burst them wide

Suddenly on the ocean's chilly streams.
The planet orb of fire, whereon he rode
270 Each day from east to west the heavens through,
Spun round in sable curtaining of clouds;
Not therefore veilèd quite, blindfold, and hid,
But ever and anon the glancing spheres,
Circles, and arcs, and broad-belting colure,
Glowed through, and wrought upon the muffling dark
Sweet-shapèd lightnings from the nadir deep
Up to the zenith,—hieroglyphics old
Which sages and keen-eyed astrologers
Then living on the earth, with labouring thought
280 Won from the gaze of many centuries:
Now lost, save what we find on remnants huge
Of stone, or marble swart; their import gone,
Their wisdom long since fled.—Two wings this orb
Possessed for glory, two fair argent wings,
Ever exalted at the God's approach:
And now, from forth the gloom their plumes immense
Rose, one by one, till all outspreaded were;
While still the dazzling globe maintained eclipse,
Awaiting for Hyperion's command.
290 Fain would he have commanded, fain took throne
And bid the day begin, if but for change.
He might not:—No, though a primeval God:
The sacred seasons might not be disturbed.
Therefore the operations of the dawn
Stayed in their birth, even as here 'tis told.
Those silver wings expanded sisterly,
Eager to sail their orb; the porches wide
Opened upon the dusk demesnes of night;
And the bright Titan, phrenzied with new woes,
300 Unused to bend, by hard compulsion bent
His spirit to the sorrow of the time;
And all along a dismal rack of clouds,
Upon the boundaries of day and night,
He stretched himself in grief and radiance faint.
There as he lay, the Heaven with its stars
Looked down on him with pity, and the voice
Of Cœlus, from the universal space,
Thus whispered low and solemn in his ear.

307 **Coelus** or Uranus, father of the Titans

"O brightest of my children dear, earth-born
And sky-engendered, Son of Mysteries   310
All unrevealèd even to the powers
Which met at thy creating; at whose joys
And palpitations sweet, and pleasures soft,
I, Cœlus, wonder, how they came and whence;
And at the fruits thereof what shapes they be,
Distinct, and visible; symbols divine,
Manifestations of that beauteous life
Diffused unseen throughout eternal space:
Of these new-formed art thou, oh brightest child!
Of these, thy brethren and the Goddesses!   320
There is sad feud among ye, and rebellion
Of son against his sire. I saw him fall,
I saw my first-born tumbled from his throne!
To me his arms were spread, to me his voice
Found way from forth the thunders round his head!
Pale wox I, and in vapours hid my face.
Art thou, too, near such doom? vague fear there is:
For I have seen my sons most unlike Gods.
Divine ye were created, and divine
In sad demeanour, solemn, undisturbed,   330
Unruffled, like high Gods, ye lived and ruled:
Now I behold in you fear, hope, and wrath;
Actions of rage and passion; even as
I see them, on the mortal world beneath,
In men who die.—This is the grief, O Son!
Sad sign of ruin, sudden dismay, and fall!
Yet do thou strive; as thou art capable,
As thou canst move about, an evident God;
And canst oppose to each malignant hour
Ethereal presence:—I am but a voice;   340
My life is but the life of winds and tides,
No more than winds and tides can I avail:—
But thou canst.—Be thou therefore in the van
Of Circumstance; yea, seize the arrow's barb
Before the tense string murmur.—To the earth!
For there thou wilt find Saturn, and his woes.
Meantime I will keep watch on thy bright sun,
And of thy seasons be a careful nurse."—
Ere half this region-whisper had come down,

323 **first-born** Saturn

350 Hyperion arose, and on the stars
　　Lifted his curvèd lids, and kept them wide
　　Until it ceased; and still he kept them wide:
　　And still they were the same bright, patient stars.
　　Then with a slow incline of his broad breast,
　　Like to a diver in the pearly seas,
　　Forward he stooped over the airy shore,
　　And plunged all noiseless into the deep night.

BOOK II

　　Just at the self-same beat of Time's wide wings
　　Hyperion slid into the rustled air,
　　And Saturn gained with Thea that sad place
　　Where Cybele and the bruisèd Titans mourned.
　　It was a den where no insulting light
　　Could glimmer on their tears; where their own groans
　　They felt, but heard not, for the solid roar
　　Of thunderous waterfalls and torrents hoarse,
　　Pouring a constant bulk, uncertain where.
10　Crag jutting forth to crag, and rocks that seemed
　　Ever as if just rising from a sleep,
　　Forehead to forehead held their monstrous horns;
　　And thus in thousand hugest phantasies
　　Made a fit roofing to this nest of woe.
　　Instead of thrones, hard flint they sat upon,
　　Couches of rugged stone, and slaty ridge
　　Stubborned with iron. All were not assembled:
　　Some chained in torture, and some wandering.
　　Cœus, and Gyges, and Briareüs,
20　Typhon, and Dolor, and Porphyrion,
　　With many more, the brawniest in assault,
　　Were pent in regions of laborious breath;
　　Dungeoned in opaque element, to keep
　　Their clenchèd teeth still clenched, and all their limbs
　　Locked up like veins of metal, crampt and screwed;
　　Without a motion, save of their big hearts
　　Heaving in pain, and horribly convulsed
　　With sanguine feverous boiling gurge of pulse.

　　4 Cybele or Ops, wife of Saturn

Mnemosyne was straying in the world;
Far from her moon had Phœbe wandered;   30
And many else were free to roam abroad,
But for the main, here found they covert drear.
Scarce images of life, one here, one there,
Lay vast and edgeways; like a dismal cirque
Of Druid stones, upon a forlorn moor,
When the chill rain begins at shut of eve,
In dull November, and their chancel vault,
The Heaven itself, is blinded throughout night.
Each one kept shroud, nor to his neighbour gave
Or word, or look, or action of despair.   40
Creüs was one; his ponderous iron mace
Lay by him, and a shattered rib of rock
Told of his rage, ere he thus sank and pined.
Iäpetus another; in his grasp,
A serpent's plashy neck; its barbèd tongue
Squeezed from the gorge, and all its uncurled length
Dead; and because the creature could not spit
Its poison in the eyes of conquering Jove.
Next Cottus: prone he lay, chin uppermost,
As though in pain; for still upon the flint   50
He ground severe his skull, with open mouth
And eyes at horrid working. Nearest him
Asia, born of most enormous Caf,
Who cost her mother Tellus keener pangs,
Though feminine, than any of her sons:
More thought than woe was in her dusky face,
For she was prophesying of her glory;
And in her wide imagination stood
Palm-shaded temples, and high rival fanes,
By Oxus or in Ganges' sacred isles.   60
Even as Hope upon her anchor leans,
So leant she, not so fair, upon a tusk
Shed from the broadest of her elephants.
Above her, on a crag's uneasy shelve,
Upon his elbow raised, all prostrate else,
Shadowed Enceladus; once tame and mild
As grazing ox unworried in the meads;
Now tiger-passioned, lion-thoughted, wroth,

29 Mnemosyne goddess of memory **39 shroud** veiled **66 Encela-
dus** a giant, son of Coelus

He meditated, plotted, and even now
70 Was hurling mountains in that second war,
Not long delayed, that scared the younger Gods
To hide themselves in forms of beast and bird.
Not far hence Atlas; and beside him prone
Phorcus, the sire of Gorgons. Neighboured close
Oceanus, and Tethys, in whose lap
Sobbed Clymene among her tangled hair.
In midst of all lay Themis, at the feet
Of Ops the queen all clouded round from sight;
No shape distinguishable, more than when
80 Thick night confounds the pine-tops with the clouds:
And many else whose names may not be told.
For when the Muse's wings are air-ward spread,
Who shall delay her flight? And she must chaunt
Of Saturn, and his guide, who now had climbed
With damp and slippery footing from a depth
More horrid still. Above a sombre cliff
Their heads appeared, and up their stature grew
Till on the level height their steps found ease:
Then Thea spread abroad her trembling arms
90 Upon the precincts of this nest of pain,
And sidelong fixed her eye on Saturn's face:
There saw she direst strife; the supreme God
At war with all the frailty of grief,
Of rage, of fear, anxiety, revenge,
Remorse, spleen, hope, but most of all despair.
Against these plagues he strove in vain; for Fate
Had poured a mortal oil upon his head,
A disanointing poison: so that Thea,
Affrighted, kept her still, and let him pass
100 First onwards in, among the fallen tribe.

As with us mortal men, the laden heart
Is persecuted more, and fevered more,
When it is nighing to the mournful house
Where other hearts are sick of the same bruise;
So Saturn, as he walked into the midst,
Felt faint, and would have sunk among the rest,
But that he met Enceladus's eye,
Whose mightiness, and awe of him, at once

75 **Oceanus** god of ocean, displaced by Neptune

Came like an inspiration; and he shouted,
"Titans, behold your God!" at which some groaned;   110
Some started on their feet; some also shouted;
Some wept, some wailed, all bowed with reverence;
And Ops, uplifting her black folded veil,
Showed her pale cheeks, and all her forehead wan,
Her eye-brows thin and jet, and hollow eyes.
There is a roaring in the bleak-grown pines
When Winter lifts his voice; there is a noise
Among immortals when a God gives sign,
With hushing finger, how he means to load
His tongue with the full weight of utterless thought,   120
With thunder, and with music, and with pomp:
Such noise is like the roar of bleak-grown pines:
Which, when it ceases in this mountained world,
No other sound succeeds; but ceasing here,
Among these fallen, Saturn's voice therefrom
Grew up like organ, that begins anew
Its strain, when other harmonies, stopt short,
Leave the dinned air vibrating silverly.
Thus grew it up—"Not in my own sad breast,
Which is its own great judge and searcher out,   130
Can I find reason why ye should be thus:
Not in the legends of the first of days,
Studied from that old spirit-leavèd book
Which starry Uranus with finger bright
Saved from the shores of darkness, when the waves
Low-ebbed still hid it up in shallow gloom;—
And the which book ye know I ever kept
For my firm-basèd footstool:—Ah, infirm!
Not there, nor in sign, symbol, or portent
Of element, earth, water, air, and fire,—   140
At war, at peace, or inter-quarreling
One against one, or two, or three, or all
Each several one against the other three,
As fire with air loud warring when rain-floods
Drown both, and press them both against earth's face,
Where, finding sulphur, a quadruple wrath
Unhinges the poor world;—not in that strife,
Wherefrom I take strange lore, and read it deep,

134 **Uranus** or Coelus, father of the Titans, most ancient of the
gods, appeared in the first age after chaos

Can I find reason why ye should be thus:
150   No, no-where can unriddle, though I search,
And pore on Nature's universal scroll
Even to swooning, why ye, Divinities,
The first-born of all shaped and palpable Gods,
Should cower beneath what, in comparison,
Is untremendous might. Yet ye are here,
O'erwhelmed, and spurned, and battered, ye are here!
O Titans, shall I say, 'Arise!'—Ye groan:
Shall I say 'Crouch!'—Ye groan. What can I then?
O Heaven wide! O unseen parent dear!
160   What can I? Tell me, all ye brethren Gods,
How we can war, how engine our great wrath!
O speak your counsel now, for Saturn's ear
Is all a-hungered. Thou, Oceanus,
Ponderest high and deep; and in thy face
I see, astonied, that severe content
Which comes of thought and musing: give us help!"

So ended Saturn; and the God of the Sea,
Sophist and sage, from no Athenian grove,
But cogitation in his watery shades,
170   Arose, with locks not oozy, and began,
In murmurs, which his first-endeavouring tongue
Caught infant-like from the far-foamèd sands.
"O ye, whom wrath consumes! who, passion-stung,
Writhe at defeat, and nurse your agonies!
Shut up your senses, stifle up your ears,
My voice is not a bellows unto ire.
Yet listen, ye who will, whilst I bring proof
How ye, perforce, must be content to stoop:
And in the proof much comfort will I give,
180   If ye will take that comfort in its truth.
We fall by course of Nature's law, not force
Of thunder, or of Jove. Great Saturn, thou
Hast sifted well the atom-universe;
But for this reason, that thou art the King,
And only blind from sheer supremacy,
One avenue was shaded from thine eyes,
Through which I wandered to eternal truth.
And first, as thou wast not the first of powers,
So art thou not the last; it cannot be:

Thou art not the beginning nor the end.   190
From Chaos and parental Darkness came
Light, the first fruits of that intestine broil,
That sullen ferment, which for wondrous ends
Was ripening in itself. The ripe hour came,
And with it Light, and Light, engendering
Upon its own producer, forthwith touched
The whole enourmous matter into Life.
Upon that very hour, our parentage,
The Heavens and the Earth, were manifest:
Then thou first born, and we the giant race,   200
Found ourselves ruling new and beauteous realms.
Now comes the pain of truth, to whom 'tis pain;
O folly! for to bear all naked truths,
And to envisage circumstance, all calm,
That is the top of sovereignty. Mark well!
As Heaven and Earth are fairer, fairer far
Than Chaos and blank Darkness, though once chiefs;
And as we show beyond that Heaven and Earth
In form and shape compact and beautiful,
In will, in action free, companionship,   210
And thousand other signs of purer life;
So on our heels a fresh perfection treads,
A power more strong in beauty, born of us
And fated to excel us, as we pass
In glory that old Darkness: nor are we
Thereby more conquered, than by us the rule
Of shapeless Chaos. Say, doth the dull soil
Quarrel with the proud forests it hath fed,
And feedeth still, more comely than itself?
Can it deny the chiefdom of green groves?   220
Or shall the tree be envious of the dove
Because it cooeth, and hath snowy wings
To wander wherewithal and find its joys?
We are such forest-trees, and our fair boughs
Have bred forth, not pale solitary doves,
But eagles golden-feathered, who do tower
Above us in their beauty, and must reign
In right thereof; for 'tis the eternal law
That first in beauty should be first in might:
Yea, by that law, another race may drive   230
Our conquerors to mourn as we do now.

Have ye beheld the young God of the Seas,
My dispossessor? Have ye seen his face?
Have ye beheld his chariot, foamed along
By noble wingèd creatures he hath made?
I saw him on the calmèd waters scud,
With such a glow of beauty in his eyes,
That it enforced me to bid sad farewell
To all my empire: farewell sad I took,
240   And hither came, to see how dolorous fate
Had wrought upon ye; and how I might best
Give consolation in this woe extreme.
Receive the truth, and let it be your balm."

    Whether through pozed conviction, or disdain,
They guarded silence, when Oceanus
Left murmuring, what deepest thought can tell?
But so it was, none answered for a space,
Save one whom none regarded, Clymene;
And yet she answered not, only complained,
250   With hectic lips, and eyes up-looking mild,
Thus wording timidly among the fierce:
"O Father, I am here the simplest voice,
And all my knowledge is that joy is gone,
And this thing woe crept in among our hearts,
There to remain for ever, as I fear:
I would not bode of evil, if I thought
So weak a creature could turn off the help
Which by just right should come of mighty Gods;
Yet let me tell my sorrow, let me tell
260   Of what I heard, and how it made me weep,
And know that we had parted from all hope.
I stood upon a shore, a pleasant shore,
Where a sweet clime was breathèd from a land
Of fragrance, quietness, and trees, and flowers.
Full of calm joy it was, as I of grief;
Too full of joy and soft delicious warmth;
So that I felt a movement in my heart
To chide, and to reproach that solitude
With songs of misery, music of our woes;
270   And sat me down, and took a mouthèd shell
And murmured into it, and made melody—

248 Clymene a sea nymph

O melody no more! for while I sang,
And with poor skill let pass into the breeze
The dull shell's echo, from a bowery strand
Just opposite, an island of the sea,
There came enchantment with the shifting wind,
That did both drown and keep alive my ears.
I threw my shell away upon the sand,
And a wave filled it, as my sense was filled
With that new blissful golden melody.   280
A living death was in each gush of sounds,
Each family of rapturous hurried notes,
That fell, one after one, yet all at once,
Like pearl beads dropping sudden from their string:
And then another, then another strain,
Each like a dove leaving its olive perch,
With music winged instead of silent plumes,
To hover round my head, and make me sick
Of joy and grief at once. Grief overcame,
And I was stopping up my frantic ears,   290
When, past all hindrance of my trembling hands,
A voice came sweeter, sweeter than all tune,
And still it cried, 'Apollo! young Apollo!
The morning-bright Apollo! young Apollo!'
I fled, it followed me, and cried 'Apollo!'
O Father, and O Brethren, had ye felt
Those pains of mine; O Saturn, hadst thou felt,
Ye would not call this too indulgèd tongue
Presumptuous, in thus venturing to be heard."

    So far her voice flowed on, like timorous brook   300
That, lingering along a pebbled coast,
Doth fear to meet the sea: but sea it met,
And shuddered; for the overwhelming voice
Of huge Enceladus swallowed it in wrath:
The ponderous syllables, like sullen waves
In the half-glutted hollows of reef-rocks,
Came booming thus, while still upon his arm
He leaned; not rising, from supreme contempt.
"Or shall we listen to the over-wise,
Or to the over-foolish, Giant-Gods?   310
Not thunderbolt on thunderbolt, till all
That rebel Jove's whole armoury were spent,

Not world on world upon these shoulders piled,
Could agonize me more than baby-words
In midst of this dethronement horrible.
Speak! roar! shout! yell! ye sleepy Titans all.
Do ye forget the blows, the buffets vile?
Are ye not smitten by a youngling arm?
Dost thou forget, sham Monarch of the Waves,
320   Thy scalding in the seas? What, have I roused
Your spleens with so few simple words as these?
O joy! for now I see ye are not lost:
O joy! for now I see a thousand eyes
Wide-glaring for revenge!"—As this he said,
He lifted up his stature vast, and stood,
Still without intermission speaking thus:
"Now ye are flames, I'll tell you how to burn,
And purge the ether of our enemies;
How to feed fierce the crooked stings of fire,
330   And singe away the swollen clouds of Jove,
Stifling that puny essence in its tent.
O let him feel the evil he hath done;
For though I scorn Oceanus's lore,
Much pain have I for more than loss of realms:
The days of peace and slumberous calm are fled;
Those days, all innocent of scathing war,
When all the fair Existences of heaven
Came open-eyed to guess what we would speak:—
That was before our brows were taught to frown.
340   Before our lips knew else but solemn sounds;
That was before we knew the wingèd thing,
Victory, might be lost, or might be won.
And be ye mindful that Hyperion,
Our brightest brother, still is undisgraced—
Hyperion, lo! his radiance is here!"

All eyes were on Enceladus's face,
And they beheld, while still Hyperion's name
Flew from his lips up to the vaulted rocks,
A pallid gleam across his features stern:
350   Not savage, for he saw full many a God
Wroth as himself. He looked upon them all,
And in each face he saw a gleam of light,
But splendider in Saturn's, whose hoar locks

Shone like the bubbling foam about a keel
When the prow sweeps into a midnight cove.
In pale and silver silence they remained,
Till suddenly a splendour, like the morn,
Pervaded all the beetling gloomy steeps,
All the sad spaces of oblivion,
And every gulf, and every chasm old,   360
And every height, and every sullen depth,
Voiceless, or hoarse with loud tormented streams:
And all the everlasting cataracts,
And all the headlong torrents far and near,
Mantled before in darkness and huge shade,
Now saw the light and made it terrible.
It was Hyperion:—a granite peak
His bright feet touched, and there he stayed to view
The misery his brilliance had betrayed
To the most hateful seeing of itself.   370
Golden his hair of short Numidian curl,
Regal his shape majestic, a vast shade
In midst of his own brightness, like the bulk
Of Memnon's image at the set of sun
To one who travels from the dusking East:
Sighs, too, as mournful as that Memnon's harp
He uttered, while his hands contemplative
He pressed together, and in silence stood.
Despondence seized again the fallen Gods
At sight of the dejected King of Day,   380
And many hid their faces from the light:
But fierce Enceladus sent forth his eyes
Among the brotherhood; and, at their glare,
Uprose Iäpetus, and Creüs too,
And Phorcus, sea-born, and together strode
To where he towered on his eminence.
There those four shouted forth old Saturn's name;
Hyperion from the peak loud answered, "Saturn!"
Saturn sat near the Mother of the Gods,
In whose face was no joy, though all the Gods   390
Gave from their hollow throats the name of "Saturn!"

358 **beetling** overhanging 374 **Memnon's image** statue in Egypt
which gave forth music when struck by the sun's rays

BOOK III

THUS in alternate uproar and sad peace,
Amazèd were those Titans utterly.
O leave them, Muse! O leave them to their woes;
For thou art weak to sing such tumults dire:
A solitary sorrow best befits
Thy lips, and antheming a lonely grief.
Leave them, O Muse! for thou anon wilt find
Many a fallen old Divinity
Wandering in vain about bewildered shores.
10   Meantime touch piously the Delphic harp,
And not a wind of heaven but will breathe
In aid soft warble from the Dorian flute;
For lo! 'tis for the Father of all verse.
Flush every thing that hath a vermeil hue,
Let the rose glow intense and warm the air,
And let the clouds of even and of morn
Float in voluptuous fleeces o'er the hills;
Let the red wine within the goblet boil,
Cold as a bubbling well; let faint-lipped shells,
20   On sands, or in great deeps, vermilion turn
Through all their labyrinths; and let the maid
Blush keenly, as with some warm kiss surprised.
Chief isle of the embowered Cyclades,
Rejoice, O Delos, with thine olives green,
And poplars, and lawn-shading palms, and beech,
In which the Zephyr breathes the loudest song,
And hazels thick, dark-stemmed beneath the shade:
Apollo is once more the golden theme!
Where was he, when the Giant of the Sun
30   Stood bright, amid the sorrow of his peers?
Together had he left his mother fair
And his twin-sister sleeping in their bower,
And in the morning twilight wandered forth
Beside the osiers of a rivulet,
Full ankle-deep in lillies of the vale.
The nightingale had ceased, and a few stars
Were lingering in the heavens, while the thrush

13 **Father** Apollo, son of Jupiter, became god of light, youth, beauty, and was associated with music and poetry 24 **Delos** island on which Apollo was born

Began calm-throated. Throughout all the isle
There was no covert, no retirèd cave
Unhaunted by the murmurous noise of waves,   40
Though scarcely heard in many a green recess.
He listened, and he wept, and his bright tears
Went trickling down the golden bow he held.
Thus with half-shut suffusèd eyes he stood,
While from beneath some cumbrous boughs hard by
With solemn step an awful Goddess came,
And there was purport in her looks for him,
Which he with eager guess began to read
Perplexed, the while melodiously he said:
"How cam'st thou over the unfooted sea?   50
Or hath that antique mien and robèd form
Moved in these vales invisible till now?
Sure I have heard those vestments sweeping o'er
The fallen leaves, when I have sat alone
In cool mid-forest. Surely I have traced
The rustle of those ample skirts about
These grassy solitudes, and seen the flowers
Lift up their heads, as still the whisper passed.
Goddess! I have beheld those eyes before,
And their eternal calm, and all that face,   60
Or I have dreamed."—"Yes," said the supreme shape,
"Thou hast dreamed of me; and awaking up
Didst find a lyre all golden by thy side,
Whose strings touched by thy fingers, all the vast
Unwearied ear of the whole universe
Listened in pain and pleasure at the birth
Of such new tuneful wonder. Is't not strange
That thou shouldst weep, so gifted? Tell me, youth,
What sorrow thou canst feel; for I am sad
When thou dost shed a tear: explain thy griefs   70
To one who in this lonely isle hath been
The watcher of thy sleep and hours of life,
From the young day when first thy infant hand
Plucked witless the weak flowers, till thine arm
Could bend that bow heroic to all times.
Show thy heart's secret to an ancient Power
Who hath forsaken old and sacred thrones

76 **ancient Power** Mnemosyne, goddess of memory, had **forsaken** the Titans

For prophecies of thee, and for the sake
Of loveliness new born."—Apollo then,
80   With sudden scrutiny and gloomless eyes,
Thus answered, while his white melodious throat
Throbbed with the syllables.—"Mnemosyne!
Thy name is on my tongue, I know not how;
Why should I tell thee what thou so well seest?
Why should I strive to show what from thy lips
Would come no mystery? For me, dark, dark,
And painful vile oblivion seals my eyes:
I strive to search wherefore I am so sad,
Until a melancholy numbs my limbs;
90   And then upon the grass I sit, and moan,
Like one who once had wings.—O why should I
Feel cursed and thwarted, when the liegeless air
Yields to my step aspirant? why should I
Spurn the green turf as hateful to my feet?
Goddess benign, point forth some unknown thing:
Are there not other regions than this isle?
What are the stars? There is the sun, the sun!
And the most patient brilliance of the moon!
And stars by thousands! Point me out the way
100   To any one particular beauteous star,
And I will flit into it with my lyre,
And make its silvery splendour pant with bliss.
I have heard the cloudy thunder: Where is power?
Whose hand, whose essence, what divinity
Makes this alarum in the elements,
While I here idle listen on the shores
In fearless yet in aching ignorance?
O tell me, lonely Goddess, by thy harp,
That waileth every morn and eventide,
110   Tell me why thus I rave, about these groves!
Mute thou remainest—mute! yet I can read
A wondrous lesson in thy silent face:
Knowledge enormous makes a God of me.
Names, deeds, grey legends, dire events, rebellions,
Majesties, sovran voices, agonies,
Creations and destroyings, all at once
Pour into the wide hollows of my brain,
And deify me, as if some blithe wine
Or bright elixir peerless I had drunk,

And so become immortal."—Thus the God,   **120**
While his enkindled eyes, with level glance
Beneath his white soft temples, stedfast kept
Trembling with light upon Mnemosyne.
Soon wild commotions shook him, and made flush
All the immortal fairness of his limbs;
Most like the struggle at the gate of death;
Or liker still to one who should take leave
Of pale immortal death, and with a pang
As hot as death's is chill, with fierce convulse
Die into life: so young Apollo anguished: **130**
His very hair, his golden tresses famed
Kept undulation round his eager neck.
During the pain Mnemosyne upheld
Her arms as one who prophesied.—At length
Apollo shrieked;—and lo! from all his limbs
Celestial   ❋   ❋   ❋   ❋   ❋   ❋   ❋
❋   ❋   ❋   ❋   ❋   ❋   ❋   ❋   ❋

1819   *1820*

The Eve of St. Agnes

Sᴛ. Agnes' Eve—Ah, bitter chill it was!
The owl, for all his feathers, was a-cold;
The hare limped trembling through the frozen grass,
And silent was the flock in woolly fold:
Numb were the Beadsman's fingers, while he told
His rosary, and while his frosted breath,
Like pious incense from a censer old,
Seemed taking flight for heaven, without a death,
Past the sweet Virgin's picture, while his prayer he saith.

His prayer he saith, this patient, holy man;   1ᴏ
Then takes his lamp, and riseth from his knees,
And back returneth, meagre, barefoot, wan,

136 In one manuscript, the last line of the fragment is completed
thus: "Celestial Glory dawned: he was a god!" 1 St. Agnes' Eve
January 20th 5 Beadsman cleric employed to pray for the souls
of his benefactors

Along the chapel aisle by slow degrees:
The sculptured dead, on each side, seem to freeze,
Emprisoned in black, purgatorial rails:
Knights, ladies, praying in dumb orat'ries,
He passeth by; and his weak spirit fails
To think how they may ache in icy hoods and mails.

Northward he turneth through a little door,
20   And scarce three steps, ere Music's golden tongue
Flattered to tears this agèd man and poor;
But no—already had his deathbell rung;
The joys of all his life were said and sung:
His was harsh penance on St. Agnes' Eve:
Another way he went, and soon among
Rough ashes sat he for his soul's reprieve,
And all night kept awake, for sinners' sake to grieve.

That ancient Beadsman heard the prelude soft;
And so it chanced, for many a door was wide,
30   From hurry to and fro. Soon, up aloft,
The silver, snarling trumpets 'gan to chide:
The level chambers, ready with their pride,
Were glowing to receive a thousand guests:
The carvèd angels, ever eager-eyed,
Stared, where upon their heads the cornice rests,
With hair blown back, and wings put cross-wise on their
     breasts.

At length burst in the argent revelry,
With plume, tiara, and all rich array,
Numerous as shadows haunting fairily
40   The brain, new stuffed, in youth, with triumphs gay
Of old romance. These let us wish away,
And turn, sole-thoughted, to one Lady there,
Whose heart had brooded, all that wintry day,
On love, and winged St. Agnes' saintly care,
As she had heard old dames full many times declare.

They told her how, upon St. Agnes' Eve,
Young virgins might have visions of delight,

15 **Emprisoned . . . rails** fenced in by iron railings, suggestive here
of prison bars 16 **dumb orat'ries** silent places of prayer

And soft adorings from their loves receive
Upon the honeyed middle of the night,
If ceremonies due they did aright;   50
As, supperless to bed they must retire,
And couch supine their beauties, lily white;
Nor look behind, nor sideways, but require
Of Heaven with upward eyes for all that they desire.

Full of this whim was thoughtful Madeline:
The music, yearning like a God in pain,
She scarcely heard: her maiden eyes divine,
Fixed on the floor, saw many a sweeping train
Pass by—she heeded not at all: in vain
Came many a tiptoe, amorous cavalier,   60
And back retired; not cooled by high disdain,
But she saw not: her heart was otherwhere:
She sighed for Agnes' dreams, the sweetest of the year.

She danced along with vague, regardless eyes,
Anxious her lips, her breathing quick and short:
The hallowed hour was near at hand: she sighs
Amid the timbrels, and the thronged resort
Of whisperers in anger, or in sport;
'Mid looks of love, defiance, hate, and scorn,
Hoodwinked with faery fancies; all amort,   70
Save to St. Agnes and her lambs unshorn,
And all the bliss to be before to-morrow morn.

So, purposing each moment to retire,
She lingered still. Meantime, across the moors,
Had come young Porphyro, with heart on fire

55 Keats originally included another stanza at this point, but was
persuaded not to publish it. The missing stanza helps to explain
later sections of the poem.
        'Twas said her future lord would there appear
        Offering as sacrifice—all in the dream—
        Delicious food even to her lips brought near:
        Viands and wine and fruit and sugared cream,
        To touch her palate with the fine extreme
        Of relish: then soft music heard; and then
        More pleasures followed in a dizzy stream
        Palpable almost: then to wake again
        Warm in the virgin morn, no weeping Magdalen.
70 **amort** unconscious

For Madeline. Beside the portal doors,
Buttressed from moonlight, stands he, and implores
All saints to give him sight of Madeline,
But for one moment in the tedious hours,
80   That he might gaze and worship all unseen;
Perchance speak, kneel, touch, kiss—in sooth such things
    have been.

He ventures in: let no buzzed whisper tell:
All eyes be muffled, or a hundred swords
Will storm his heart, Love's fev'rous citadel:
For him, those chambers held barbarian hordes,
Hyena foemen, and hot-blooded lords,
Whose very dogs would execrations howl
Against his lineage: not one breast affords
Him any mercy, in that mansion foul,
90   Save one old beldame, weak in body and in soul.

Ah, happy chance! the agèd creature came,
Shuffling along with ivory-headed wand,
To where he stood, hid from the torch's flame,
Behind a broad hall-pillar, far beyond
The sound of merriment and chorus bland:
He startled her; but soon she knew his face,
And grasped his fingers in her palsied hand,
Saying, "Mercy, Porphyro! hie thee from this place;
They are all here to-night, the whole blood-thirsty race!

100   "Get hence! get hence! there's dwarfish Hildebrand;
He had a fever late, and in the fit
He cursèd thee and thine, both house and land:
Then there's that old Lord Maurice, not a whit
More tame for his gray hairs—Alas me! flit!
Flit like a ghost away."—"Ah, Gossip dear,
We're safe enough; here in this arm-chair sit,
And tell me how"—"Good Saints! not here, not here;
Follow me, child, or else these stones will be thy bier."

He followed through a lowly archèd way,
110   Brushing the cobwebs with his lofty plume,
And as she muttered "Well-a—well-a-day!"
He found him in a little moonlight room,

90 **beldame** aged woman   105 **Gossip** old friend

Pale, latticed, chill, and silent as a tomb.
"Now tell me where is Madeline," said he,
"O tell me, Angela, by the holy loom
Which none but secret sisterhood may see,
When they St. Agnes' wool are weaving piously."

"St. Agnes! Ah! it is St. Agnes' Eve—
Yet men will murder upon holy days:
Thou must hold water in a witch's sieve,   120
And be liege-lord of all the Elves and Fays,
To venture so: it fills me with amaze
To see thee, Porphyro!—St. Agnes' Eve!
God's help! my lady fair the conjuror plays
This very night: good angels her deceive!
But let me laugh awhile, I've mickle time to grieve."

Feebly she laugheth in the languid moon,
While Porphyro upon her face doth look,
Like puzzled urchin on an agèd crone
Who keepeth closed a wond'rous riddle-book,   130
As spectacled she sits in chimney nook.
But soon his eyes grew brilliant, when she told
His lady's purpose; and he scarce could brook
Tears, at the thought of those enchantments cold,
And Madeline asleep in lap of legends old.

Sudden a thought came like a full-blown rose,
Flushing his brow, and in his painèd heart
Made purple riot: then doth he propose
A strategem, that makes the beldame start:
"A cruel man and impious thou art: 140
Sweet lady, let her pray, and sleep, and dream
Alone with her good angels, far apart
From wicked men like thee. Go, go!—I deem
Thou canst not surely be the same that thou didst seem."

"I will not harm her, by all saints I swear,"
Quoth Porphyro: "O may I ne'er find grace
When my weak voice shall whisper its last prayer,
If one of her soft ringlets I displace,
Or look with ruffian passion in her face:
Good Angela, believe me by these tears;   150

126 mickle much

Or I will, even in a moment's space,
Awake, with horrid shout, my foemen's ears,
And beard them, though they be more fanged than wolves
    and bears."

"Ah! why wilt thou affright a feeble soul?
A poor, weak, palsy-stricken, churchyard thing,
Whose passing-bell may ere the midnight toll;
Whose prayers for thee, each morn and evening,
Were never missed."—Thus plaining, doth she bring
A gentler speech from burning Porphyro;
160   So woful, and of such deep sorrowing,
That Angela gives promise she will do
Whatever he shall wish, betide her weal or woe.

Which was, to lead him, in close secrecy,
Even to Madeline's chamber, and there hide
Him in a closet, of such privacy
That he might see her beauty unespied,
And win perhaps that night a peerless bride,
While legioned fairies paced the coverlet,
And pale enchantment held her sleepy-eyed.
170   Never on such a night have lovers met,
Since Merlin paid his Demon all the monstrous debt.

"It shall be as thou wishest," said the Dame:
"All cates and dainties shall be storèd there
Quickly on this feast-night: by the tambour frame
Her own lute thou wilt see: no time to spare,
For I am slow and feeble, and scarce dare
On such a catering trust my dizzy head.
Wait here, my child, with patience; kneel in prayer
The while: Ah! thou must needs the lady wed,
180 Or may I never leave my grave among the dead."

So saying, she hobbled off with busy fear.
The lover's endless minutes slowly passed;
The dame returned, and whispered in his ear
To follow her; with agèd eyes aghast
From fright of dim espial. Safe at last,

158 **plaining** lamenting   171 **Merlin . . . debt** Merlin, the magi-
cian, was created by a demon and was later destroyed   173 **cates**
provisions

Through many a dusky gallery, they gain
The maiden's chamber, silken, hushed, and chaste;
Where Porphyro took covert, pleased amain.
His poor guide hurried back with agues in her brain.

Her falt'ring hand upon the balustrade,   190
Old Angela was feeling for the stair,
When Madeline, St. Agnes' charmèd maid,
Rose, like a missioned spirit, unaware:
With silver taper's light, and pious care,
She turned, and down the agèd gossip led
To a safe level matting. Now prepare,
Young Porphyro, for gazing on that bed;
She comes, she comes again, like ring-dove frayed and fled.

Out went the taper as she hurried in;
Its little smoke, in pallid moonshine, died: 200
She closed the door, she panted, all akin
To spirits of the air, and visions wide:
No uttered syllable, or, woe betide!
But to her heart, her heart was voluble,
Paining with eloquence her balmy side;
As though a tongueless nightingale should swell
Her throat in vain, and die, heart-stifled, in her dell.

A casement high and triple-arched there was,
All garlanded with carven imag'ries
Of fruits, and flowers, and bunches of knot-grass,   210
And diamonded with panes of quaint device,
Innumerable of stains and splendid dyes,
As are the tiger-moth's deep-damasked wings;
And in the midst, 'mong thousand heraldries,
And twilight saints, and dim emblazonings,
A shielded scutcheon blushed with blood of queens and
        kings.

Full on this casement shone the wintry moon,
And threw warm gules on Madeline's fair breast,
As down she knelt for heaven's grace and boon;
Rose-bloom fell on her hands, together prest,   220

188 **amain** exceedingly 198 **frayed** frightened 218 **gules** red colours

And on her silver cross soft amethyst,
And on her hair a glory, like a saint:
She seemed a splendid angel, newly drest,
Save wings, for heaven:—Porphyro grew faint:
She knelt, so pure a thing, so free from mortal taint.

Anon his heart revives: her vespers done,
Of all its wreathèd pearls her hair she frees;
Unclasps her warmèd jewels one by one;
Loosens her fragrant boddice; by degrees
230 Her rich attire creeps rustling to her knees:
Half-hidden, like a mermaid in sea-weed,
Pensive awhile she dreams awake, and sees,
In fancy, fair St. Agnes in her bed,
But dares not look behind, or all the charm is fled.

Soon, trembling in her soft and chilly nest,
In sort of wakeful swoon, perplexed she lay,
Until the poppied warmth of sleep oppressed
Her soothèd limbs, and soul fatigued away;
Flown, like a thought, until the morrow-day;
240 Blissfully havened both from joy and pain;
Clasped like a missal where swart Paynims pray;
Blinded alike from sunshine and from rain,
As though a rose should shut, and be a bud again.

Stol'n to this paradise, and so entranced,
Porphyro gazed upon her empty dress,
And listened to her breathing, if it chanced
To wake into a slumberous tenderness;
Which when he heard, that minute did he bless,
And breathed himself: then from the closet crept,
250 Noiseless as fear in a wide wilderness,
And over the hushed carpet, silent, stept,
And 'tween the curtains peeped, where, lo!—how fast she
slept.

Then by the bed-side, where the faded moon
Made a dim, silver twilight, soft he set
A table, and, half anguished, threw thereon

241 **Clasped** kept tightly shut **missal** Christian prayer book **swart**
dark-skinned **Paynims** pagans

A cloth of woven crimson, gold, and jet:—
O for some drowsy Morphean amulet!
The boisterous, midnight, festive clarion,
The kettle-drum, and far-heard clarionet,
Affray his ears, though but in dying tone:—   260
The hall door shuts again, and all the noise is gone.

And still she slept an azure-lidded sleep,
In blanchèd linen, smooth, and lavendered,
While he from forth the closet brought a heap
Of candied apple, quince, and plum, and gourd,
With jellies soother than the creamy curd,
And lucent syrops, tinct with cinnamon;
Manna and dates, in argosy transferred
From Fez; and spicèd dainties, every one,
From silken Samarcand to cedared Lebanon.   270

These delicates he heaped with glowing hand
On golden dishes and in baskets bright
Of wreathèd silver: sumptuous they stand
In the retirèd quiet of the night,
Filling the chilly room with perfume light.—
"And now, my love, my seraph fair, awake!
Thou art my heaven, and I thine eremite:
Open thine eyes, for meek St. Agnes' sake,
Or I shall drowse beside thee, so my soul doth ache."

Thus whispering, his warm, unnervèd arm   280
Sank in her pillow. Shaded was her dream
By the dusk curtains:—'twas a midnight charm
Impossible to melt as icèd stream:
The lustrous salvers in the moonlight gleam;
Broad golden fringe upon the carpet lies:
It seemed he never, never could redeem
From such a stedfast spell his lady's eyes;
So mused awhile, entoiled in woofèd phantasies.

Awakening up, he took her hollow lute,—
Tumultuous,—and, in chords that tenderest be,   290
He played an ancient ditty, long since mute,

257 **Morphean** of Morpheus, god of sleep **amulet** magic charm
266 **soother** more soothing 277 **eremite** hermit or worshipper

In Provence called, "La belle dame sans mercy:"
Close to her ear touching the melody;—
Wherewith disturbed, she uttered a soft moan:
He ceased—she panted quick—and suddenly
Her blue affrayèd eyes wide open shone:
Upon his knees he sank, pale as smooth-sculptured stone.

Her eyes were open, but she still beheld,
Now wide awake, the vision of her sleep:
300   There was a painful change, that nigh expelled
The blisses of her dream so pure and deep
At which fair Madeline began to weep,
And moan forth witless words with many a sigh;
While still her gaze on Porphyro would keep;
Who knelt, with joinèd hands and piteous eye,
Fearing to move or speak, she looked so dreamingly.

"Ah, Porphyro!" said she, "but even now
Thy voice was at sweet tremble in mine ear,
Made tuneable with every sweetest vow;
310   And those sad eyes were spiritual and clear:
How changed thou art! how pallid, chill, and drear!
Give me that voice again, my Porphyro,
Those looks immortal, those complainings dear!
Oh leave me not in this eternal woe,
For if thou diest, my Love, I know not where to go."

Beyond a mortal man impassioned far
At these voluptuous accents, he arose,
Ethereal, flushed, and like a throbbing star
Seen mid the sapphire heaven's deep repose
320   Into her dream he melted, as the rose
Blendeth its odour with the violet,—
Solution sweet: meantime the frost-wind blows
Like Love's alarum pattering the sharp sleet
Against the window-panes; St. Agnes' moon hath set.

'Tis dark: quick pattereth the flaw-blown sleet:
"This is no dream, my bride, my Madeline!"
'Tis dark: the icèd gusts still rave and beat:
"No dream, alas! alas! and woe is mine!
Porphyro will leave me here to fade and pine.

Cruel! what traitor could thee hither bring? 330
I curse not, for my heart is lost in thine
Though thou forsakest a deceivèd thing;—
A dove forlorn and lost with sick unprunèd wing."

"My Madeline! sweet dreamer! lovely bride!
Say, may I be for aye thy vassal blest?
Thy beauty's shield, heart-shaped and vermeil dyed?
Ah, silver shrine, here will I take my rest
After so many hours of toil and quest,
A famished pilgrim,—saved by miracle.
Though I have found, I will not rob thy nest 340
Saving of thy sweet self; if thou think'st well
To trust, fair Madeline, to no rude infidel.

"Hark! 'tis an elfin-storm from faery land,
Of haggard seeming, but a boon indeed:
Arise—arise! the morning is at hand;—
The bloated wassaillers will never heed:—
Let us away, my love, with happy speed;
There are no ears to hear, or eyes to see,—
Drowned all in Rhenish and the sleepy mead:
Awake! arise! my love, and fearless be, 350
For o'er the southern moors I have a home for thee."

She hurried at his words, beset with fears,
For there were sleeping dragons all around,
At glaring watch, perhaps, with ready spears—
Down the wide stairs a darkling way they found.—
In all the house was heard no human sound.
A chain-drooped lamp was flickering by each door;
The arras, rich with horseman, hawk, and hound,
Fluttered in the besieging wind's uproar;
And the long carpets rose along the gusty floor. 360

They glide, like phantoms, into the wide hall;
Like phantoms, to the iron porch, they glide;
Where lay the Porter, in uneasy sprawl,
With a huge empty flaggon by his side:
The wakeful bloodhound rose, and shook his hide,
But his sagacious eye an inmate owns:

344 haggard wild

By one, and one, the bolts full easy slide:—
The chains lie silent on the footworn stones;—
The key turns, and the door upon its hinges groans.

370   And they are gone: ay, ages long ago
These lovers fled away into the storm.
That night the Baron dreamt of many a woe,
And all his warrior-guests, with shade and form
Of witch, and demon, and large coffin-worm,
Were long be-nightmared. Angela the old
Died palsy-twitched, with meagre face deform;
The Beadsman, after thousand aves told,
For aye unsought for slept among his ashes cold.

1819   *1820*

To Fanny

PHYSICIAN Nature! let my spirit blood!
   O ease my heart of verse and let me rest;
Throw me upon thy Tripod, till the flood
   Of stifling numbers ebbs from my full breast.
A theme! a theme! great nature! give a theme;
     Let me begin my dream.
I come—I see thee, as thou standest there,
Beckon me out into the wintry air.

Ah! dearest love, sweet home of all my fears,
10   And hopes, and joys, and panting miseries,—
To-night, if I may guess, thy beauty wears
     A smile of such delight,
     As brilliant and as bright,
As when with ravished, aching, vassal eyes,
     Lost in soft amaze,
     I gaze, I gaze!

Title addressed as an ode to Frances Brawne, the name Fanny being a common abbreviation for Frances 1 **Physician . . . blood** ref. to former surgical treatment of high blood-pressure etc. by letting off some of the patient's blood. Here the pressure is of the spirit, the emotional pressure of jealousy occasioned by Fanny Brawne attending a dance while Keats was ill 3 **Tripod** three-legged vessel associated with sacrificial rites

Who now, with greedy looks, eats up my feast?
　What stare outfaces now my silver moon!
Ah! keep that hand unravished at the least;
　　　Let, let, the amorous burn— 20
　　　But, pr'ythee, do not turn
　The current of your heart from me so soon.
　　　O! save, in charity,
　　　The quickest pulse for me.

Save it for me, sweet love! though music breathe
　Voluptuous visions into the warm air;
Though swimming through the dance's dangerous wreath;
　　　Be like an April day,
　　　Smiling and cold and gay,
　A temperate lily, temperate as fair; 30
　　　Then, Heaven! there will be
　　　A warmer June for me.

Why, this—you'll say, my Fanny! is not true:
　Put your soft hand upon your snowy side,
Where the heart beats: confess—'tis nothing new—
　　　Must not a woman be
　　　A feather on the sea,
　Swayed to and fro by every wind and tide?
　　　Of as uncertain speed
　　　As blow-ball from the mead? 40

I know it—and to know it is despair
　To one who loves you as I love, sweet Fanny!
Whose heart goes fluttering for you every where,
　　　Nor, when away you roam,
　　　Dare keep its wretched home,
　Love, Love alone, his pains severe and many:
　　　Then, loveliest! keep me free,
　　　From torturing jealousy.

Ah! if you prize my subdued soul above
　The poor, the fading, brief, pride of an hour; 50
Let none profane my Holy See of love,
　　　Or with a rude hand break
　　　The sacramental cake:

51 See sanctuary

Let none else touch the just new-budded flower;
  If not—may my eyes close,
  Love! on their last repose.

1819   *1848*

The Eve of Saint Mark

UPON a Sabbath-day it fell;
Twice holy was the Sabbath-bell,
That called the folk to evening prayer;
The city streets were clean and fair
From wholesome drench of April rains;
And, on the western window panes,
The chilly sunset faintly told
Of unmatured green vallies cold,
Of the green thorny bloomless hedge,
Of rivers new with spring-tide sedge,
Of primroses by sheltered rills,
And daisies on the aguish hills.
Twice holy was the Sabbath-bell:
The silent streets were crowded well
With staid and pious companies,
Warm from their fire-side orat'ries;
And moving, with demurest air,
To even-song, and vesper prayer.
Each archèd porch, and entry low,
Was filled with patient folk and slow,
With whispers hush, and shuffling feet,
While played the organ loud and sweet.

The bells had ceased, the prayers begun,
And Bertha had not yet half done
A curious volume, patched and torn,
That all day long, from earliest morn,
Had taken captive her two eyes,
Among its golden broideries;
Perplexed her with a thousand things,—
The stars of Heaven, and angels' wings,
Martyrs in a fiery blaze,

25 **volume** illuminated manuscript describing the lives of saints

Azure saints in silver rays,
Aaron's breastplate, and the seven
Candlesticks John saw in Heaven,
The wingèd Lion of Saint Mark,
And the Covenantal Ark,
With its many mysteries,
Cherubim and golden mice.

Bertha was a maiden fair,
Dwelling in the old Minster-square;   40
From her fire-side she could see,
Sidelong, its rich antiquity,
Far as the Bishop's garden-wall;
Where sycamores and elm-trees tall,
Full-leaved, the forest had outstript,
By no sharp north-wind ever nipt,
So sheltered by the mighty pile.
Bertha arose, and read awhile,
With forehead 'gainst the window-pane.
Again she tried, and then again,   50
Until the dusk eve left her dark
Upon the legend of St. Mark.
From plaited lawn-frill, fine and thin,
She lifted up her soft warm chin,
With aching neck and swimming eyes,
And dazed with saintly imag'ries.

All was gloom, and silent all,
Save now and then the still foot-fall
Of one returning homewards late,
Past the echoing minster-gate.   60

The clamorous daws, that all the day
Above tree-tops and towers play,
Pair by pair had gone to rest,
Each in its ancient belfry-nest,
Where asleep they fall betimes,
To music of the drowsy chimes.

All was silent, all was gloom,
Abroad and in the homely room:

33 **Aaron** see Exodus xxviii: 15 34 **Candlesticks** see Revelations
i: 12

Down she sat, poor cheated soul!
70   And struck a lamp from the dismal coal;
Leaned forward, with bright drooping hair
And slant book, full against the glare.
Her shadow, in uneasy guise,
Hovered about, a giant size,
On ceiling-beam and old oak chair,
The parrot's cage, and panel square;
And the warm angled winter screen,
On which were many monsters seen,
Called doves of Siam, Lima mice,
80   And legless birds of Paradise,
Macaw, and tender Av'davat,
And silken-furred Angora cat.
Untired she read, her shadow still
Glowered about, as it would fill
The room with wildest forms and shades,
As though some ghostly queen of spades
Had come to mock behind her back,
And dance, and ruffle her garments black.
Untired she read the legend page,
90   Of holy Mark, from youth to age,
On land, on sea, in pagan chains,
Rejoicing for his many pains.
Sometimes the learnèd eremite,
With golden star, or dagger bright,
Referred to pious poesies
Written in smallest crow-quill size
Beneath the text; and thus the rhyme
Was parcelled out from time to time:
——"Als writith he of swevenis,
100   Men han beforne they wake in bliss,
Whanne that hir friendes thinke hem bound
In crimped shroude farre under grounde;
And how a litling child mote be
A saint er its nativitie,
Gif that the modre (God her blesse!)
Kepen in solitarinesse,
And kissen devoute the holy croce.

81 **Av'davat** Indian songbird 93-4 **eremite . . . bright** the hermit
used golden asterisks to refer to footnotes 99 **swevenis** dreams
100 **han** have 101 **hir** their 105 **Gif** if **modre** mother

Of Goddes love, and Sathan's force,—
He writith; and thinges many mo:
Of swiche thinges I may not show.   110
Bot I must tellen verilie
Somdel of Saintè Cicilie,
And chieflie what he auctorethe
Of Saintè Markis life and dethe:"

At length her constant eyelids come
Upon the fervent martyrdom;
Then lastly to his holy shrine,
Exalt amid the tapers' shine
At Venice,—

1819   *1848*

La Belle Dame Sans Merci

O what can ail thee, knight-at-arms,
    Alone and palely loitering?
The sedge has withered from the lake,
    And no birds sing.

O what can ail thee, knight-at-arms!
    So haggard and so woe-begone?
The squirrel's granary is full,
    And the harvest's done.

I see a lilly on thy brow,
    With anguish moist and fever dew,   10
And on thy cheeks a fading rose
    Fast withereth too.

I met a lady in the meads,
    Full beautiful—a faery's child,
Her hair was long, her foot was light,
    And her eyes were wild.

110 **swiche** such 112 **Somdel** somewhat 13 **I met** the knight be-
gins speaking

I made a garland for her head,
    And bracelets too, and fragrant zone;
She looked at me as she did love,
20   And made sweet moan.

I set her on my pacing steed,
    And nothing else saw all day long,
For sidelong would she bend, and sing
    A faery's song.

She found me roots of relish sweet,
    And honey wild, and manna dew,
And sure in language strange she said—
    "I love thee true."

She took me to her elfin grot,
30   And there she wept, and sighed full sore,
And there I shut her wild wild eyes
    With kisses four.

And there she lullèd me asleep,
    And there I dreamed—Ah! woe betide!
The latest dream I ever dreamed
    On the cold hill side.

I saw pale kings and princes too,
    Pale warriors, death-pale were they all;
They cried—"La Belle Dame sans Merci
40   Hath thee in thrall!"

I saw their starved lips in the gloam,
    With horrid warning gapèd wide,
And I awoke and found me here,
    On the cold hill's side.

And this is why I sojourn here,
    Alone and palely loitering,
Though the sedge has withered from the lake,
    And no birds sing.

1819   *1820*

18 zone belt

[handwritten: Spirits, mind, intuitive intelligence]

[handwritten: most understandable]

Ode to Psyche

O GODDESS! hear these tuneless numbers, wrung
By sweet enforcement and remembrance dear,
And pardon that thy secrets should be sung
Even into thine own soft-conchèd ear: *[handwritten: appeal to 5 senses]*
Surely I dreamt to-day, or did I see
The wingèd Psyche with awakened eyes?
I wandered in a forest thoughtlessly,
And, on the sudden, fainting with surprise,
Saw two fair creatures, couchèd side by side
In deepest grass, beneath the whisp'ring roof   10
Of leaves and trembled blossoms, where there ran
A brooklet, scarce espied:
'Mid hushed, cool-rooted flowers, fragrant-eyed, *[handwritten: Combines 2 senses]*
Blue, silver-white, and budded Tyrian,
They lay calm-breathing on the bedded grass;
Their arms embracèd, and their pinions too;
Their lips touched not, but had not bade adieu,
As if disjoinèd by soft-handed slumber,
And ready still past kisses to outnumber
At tender eye-dawn of aurorean love: 20
The wingèd boy I knew;
But who wast thou, O happy, happy dove? *[handwritten: Psyche + Cupid]*
His Psyche true!

O latest born and loveliest vision far
Of all Olympus' faded hierarchy!
Fairer than Phœbe's sapphire-regioned star,
Or Vesper, amorous glow-worm of the sky;
Fairer than these, though temple thou hast none,
Nor altar heaped with flowers;

4 conchèd shaped like a seashell **6 Psyche** goddess of the soul,
loved by Cupid, god of love **21 wingèd boy** Cupid **24 O latest . . .
hierarchy** Keats explains in a letter: "Psyche was not embodied as
a goddess before the time of Apuleius [about 150 A.D.] and con-
sequently . . . was never worshipped or sacrificed to with any of
the ancient fervor, and perhaps never thought of in the old reli-
gion. I am more orthodox than to let a heathen goddess be so neg-
lected." **26 Phoebe** moon goddess

30   Nor virgin-choir to make delicious moan
         Upon the midnight hours;
   No voice, no lute, no pipe, no incense sweet
         From chain-swung censer teeming;
   No shrine, no grove, no oracle, no heat
         Of pale-mouthed prophet dreaming.

   O brightest! though too late for antique vows,
         Too, too late for the fond believing lyre,
   When holy were the haunted forest boughs,
         Holy the air, the water, and the fire;
40   Yet even in these days so far retired
         From happy pieties, thy lucent fans,
         Fluttering among the faint Olympians,
   I see, and sing, by my own eyes inspired.
   So let me be thy choir, and make a moan
         Upon the midnight hours;
   Thy voice, thy lute, thy pipe, thy incense sweet
         From swingèd censer teeming;
   Thy shrine, thy grove, thy oracle, thy heat
         Of pale-mouthed prophet dreaming.

50   Yes, I will be thy priest, and build a fane
   In some untrodden region of my mind,
   Where branchèd thoughts, new grown with pleasant
         pain,
   Instead of pines shall murmur in the wind:
   Far, far around shall those dark-clustered trees
         Fledge the wild-ridgèd mountains steep by steep;
   And there by zephyrs, streams, and birds, and bees,
         The moss-lain Dryads shall be lulled to sleep;
   And in the midst of this wide quietness
   A rosy sanctuary will I dress
60   With the wreathed trellis of a working brain,
         With buds, and bells, and stars without a name,
   With all the gardener Fancy e'er could feign,
         Who breeding flowers, will never breed the same:
   And there shall be for thee all soft delight
         That shadowy thought can win,

41 **fans** wings   57 **Dryads** tree nymphs

A bright torch, and a casement ope at night,
　To let the warm Love in!

1819   *1820*

Ode to a Nightingale

MY heart aches, and a drowsy numbness pains
　My sense, as though of hemlock I had drunk,
Or emptied some dull opiate to the drains
　One minute past, and Lethe-wards had sunk:
'Tis not through envy of thy happy lot,
　But being too happy in thine happiness,—
　　That thou, light-wingèd Dryad of the trees,
　　　In some melodious plot
　Of beechen green, and shadows numberless,
　　Singest of summer in full-throated ease.   10

O, for a draught of vintage! that hath been
　Cooled a long age in the deep-delvèd earth,
Tasting of Flora and the country green,
　Dance, and Provençal song, and sunburnt mirth!
O for a beaker full of the warm South,
　Full of the true, the blushful Hippocrene,
　　With beaded bubbles winking at the brim,
　　　And purple-stainèd mouth;
　That I might drink, and leave the world unseen,
　　And with thee fade away into the forest dim: 20

Fade far away, dissolve, and quite forget
　What thou among the leaves hast never known,
The weariness, the fever, and the fret
　Here, where men sit and hear each other groan;
Where palsy shakes a few, sad, last gray hairs,
　Where youth grows pale, and spectre-thin, and dies;
　　Where but to think is to be full of sorrow
　　　And leaden-eyed despairs,
　Where Beauty cannot keep her lustrous eyes,
　　Or new Love pine at them beyond to-morrow.   30

4 **Lethe** river of forgetfulness 16 **Hippocrene** a fountain whose
waters are supposed to inspire poets

Away! away! for I will fly to thee,
   Not charioted by Bacchus and his pards,
But on the viewless wings of Poesy,
   Though the dull brain perplexes and retards:
Already with thee! tender is the night,
   And haply the Queen-Moon is on her throne,
     Clustered around by all her starry Fays;
     But here there is no light,
Save what from heaven is with the breezes blown
     Through verdurous glooms and winding mossy
          ways.

gone into the forest

40

I cannot see what flowers are at my feet,
   Nor what soft incense hangs upon the boughs,
But, in embalmèd darkness, guess each sweet
   Wherewith the seasonable month endows
The grass, the thicket, and the fruit-tree wild;
   White hawthorn, and the pastoral eglantine;
     Fast fading violets covered up in leaves;
     And mid-May's eldest child,
The coming musk-rose, full of dewy wine,
     The murmurous haunt of flies on summer eves.

Imagining the seasons going on without him →

50

Darkling I listen; and, for many a time
   I have been half in love with easeful Death,
Called him soft names in many a musèd rhyme,
   To take into the air my quiet breath;
Now more than ever seems it rich to die,
   To cèase upon the midnight with no pain,
     While thou art pouring forth thy soul abroad
     In such an ecstasy!
Still wouldst thou sing, and I have ears in vain—
     To thy high requiem become a sod.

fusion of sound & sense

Thou wast not born for death, immortal Bird!
   No hungry generations tread thee down;
The voice I hear this passing night was heard
   In ancient days by emperor and clown:
Perhaps the self-same song that found a path
   Through the sad heart of Ruth, when, sick for home,

32 **Bacchus . . . pards** his chariot was drawn by leopards 51 **Darkling** in the dark

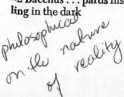

philosophical on the nature of reality

She stood in tears amid the alien corn;
　　The same that oft-times hath
Charmed magic casements, opening on the foam
　　Of perilous seas, in faery lands forlorn.   70

Forlorn! the very word is like a bell
　　To toll me back from thee to my sole self!
Adieu! the fancy cannot cheat so well
　　As she is famed to do, deceiving elf.
Adieu! adieu! thy plaintive anthem fades
　　Past the near meadows, over the still stream,
　　　Up the hill-side; and now 'tis buried deep
　　　　In the next valley-glades:
　　Was it a vision, or a waking dream?
　　　Fled is that music:—Do I wake or sleep?   80

1819   *1820*

[handwritten margin note: what is the ultimate reality?]

[handwritten margin note: (T.S. Eliot uses same in Prufrock)]

Ode on a Grecian Urn

THOU still unravished bride of quietness,
　　Thou foster-child of silence and slow time,
Sylvan historian, who canst thus express
　　A flowery tale more sweetly than our rhyme:
What leaf-fringed legend haunts about thy shape
　　Of deities or mortals, or of both,
　　　In Tempe or the dales of Arcady?
　　What men or gods are these? What maidens loth?
What mad pursuit? What struggle to escape?
　　What pipes and timbrels? What wild ecstasy?   10

[handwritten margin note: music in the mind is greater than — what is real]

Heard melodies are sweet, but those unheard
　　Are sweeter; therefore, ye soft pipes, play on;
Not to the sensual ear, but, more endeared,
　　Pipe to the spirit ditties of no tone:
Fair youth, beneath the trees, thou canst not leave
　　Thy song, nor ever can those trees be bare;
　　　Bold Lover, never, never canst thou kiss,
Though winning near the goal—yet, do not grieve;
　　She cannot fade, though thou hast not thy bliss,
　　For ever wilt thou love, and she be fair!   20

[handwritten margin note: frozen in time - never]

[handwritten margin note: consummated will never lose her]

[handwritten margin note: paradox - natures of art - unending]

Ah, happy, happy boughs! that cannot shed
    Your leaves, nor ever bid the Spring adieu;
And, happy melodist, unwearièd,
    For ever piping songs for ever new;
More happy love! more happy, happy love!
    For ever warm and still to be enjoyed,
        For ever panting, and for ever young;
All breathing human passion far above,
    That leaves a heart high-sorrowful and cloyed,
30   A burning forehead, and a parching tongue.

Who are these coming to the sacrifice?
    To what green altar, O mysterious priest,
Lead'st thou that heifer lowing at the skies,
    And all her silken flanks with garlands drest?
What little town by river or sea shore,
    Or mountain-built with peaceful citadel,
        Is emptied of this folk, this pious morn?
And, little town, thy streets for evermore
    Will silent be; and not a soul to tell
40   Why thou art desolate, can e'er return.

O Attic shape! Fair attitude! with brede
    Of marble men and maidens overwrought,
With forest branches and the trodden weed;
    Thou, silent form, dost tease us out of thought
As doth eternity: Cold Pastoral!
    When old age shall this generation waste,
        Thou shalt remain, in midst of other woe
Than ours, a friend to man, to whom thou say'st,
    "Beauty is truth, truth beauty,"—that is all
50   Ye know on earth, and all ye need to know.

1819   1820

41 **brede** interwoven pattern

Ode on Melancholy

(handwritten margin notes: — language it tries to negotiate this melancholy / sense of life / images of time & temporality)

No, no, go not to Lethe, neither twist
  Wolf's-bane, tight-rooted, for its poisonous wine;
Nor suffer thy pale forehead to be kissed
  By nightshade, ruby grape of Proserpine;
Make not your rosary of yew-berries,
  Nor let the beetle, nor the death-moth be
    Your mournful Psyche, nor the downy owl
A partner in your sorrow's mysteries;
  For shade to shade will come too drowsily,
    And drown the wakeful anguish of the soul.   10

But when the melancholy fit shall fall
  Sudden from heaven like a weeping cloud,
That fosters the droop-headed flowers all,
  And hides the green hill in an April shroud;
Then glut thy sorrow on a morning rose,
  Or on the rainbow of the salt sand-wave,
    Or on the wealth of globèd peonies;
Or if thy mistress some rich anger shows,
  Emprison her soft hand, and let her rave,
    And feed deep, deep upon her peerless eyes.   20

She dwells with Beauty—Beauty that must die;
  And Joy, whose hand is ever at his lips
Bidding adieu; and aching Pleasure nigh,
  Turning to Poison while the bee-mouth sips:
Ay, in the very temple of delight
  Veiled Melancholy has her sovran shrine,
    Though seen of none save him whose strenuous tongue
Can burst Joy's grape against his palate fine;
  His soul shall taste the sadness of her might,
    And be among her cloudy trophies hung.   30

(handwritten margin notes: both paying tribute to Beauty yet going beyond)

1819   *1820*

1 Lethe river of forgetfulness **2 Wolf's-bane** a plant **3 Nor suffer**
. . . **nightshade** nor allow your forehead to be crowned with a
wreath made of the red berries of the poisonous nightshade plant
4 Proserpine goddess from Hades **6 beetle** ancient death symbol
death-moth reference to the tradition that immediately after
death, the soul of a dead man could be seen in the form of a
butterfly fluttering above his mouth **7 Psyche** goddess of the soul,
as guardian spirit

Lamia

PART I

Upon a time, before the faery broods
Drove Nymph and Satyr from the prosperous woods,
Before king Oberon's bright diadem,
Sceptre, and mantle, clasped with dewy gem,
Frighted away the Dryads and the Fauns
From rushes green, and brakes, and cowslipped lawns,
The ever-smitten Hermes empty left
His golden throne, bent warm on amorous theft:
From high Olympus had he stolen light,
10 On this side of Jove's clouds, to escape the sight
Of his great summoner, and made retreat
Into a forest on the shores of Crete.
For somewhere in that sacred island dwelt
A nymph, to whom all hoofèd Satyrs knelt;
At whose white feet the languid Tritons poured
Pearls, while on land they withered and adored.
Fast by the springs where she to bathe was wont,
And in those meads where sometime she might haunt,
Were strewn rich gifts, unknown to any Muse,
20 Though Fancy's casket were unlocked to choose.
Ah, what a world of love was at her feet!
So Hermes thought, and a celestial heat
Burnt from his wingèd heels to either ear,
That from a whiteness, as the lilly clear,
Blushed into roses 'mid his golden hair,
Fallen in jealous curls about his shoulders bare.

From vale to vale, from wood to wood, he flew,
Breathing upon the flowers his passion new,

3 **Oberon** king of the demons or fairies. The stories of nymphs and other spirits of classical legend were later displaced in popular imagination by stories of the fairy spirits, and thus the nymphs were "frighted away." Although the setting of the poem is classical, there are many references to "faery power" in order to suggest a world of magic illusion, especially the fragile illusion of love. 5 **Dryads** tree nymphs 7 **Hermes** or Mercury, messenger of the gods 15 **Tritons** mermen

And wound with many a river to its head,
To find where this sweet nymph prepared her secret bed: 30
In vain; the sweet nymph might nowhere be found,
And so he rested, on the lonely ground,
Pensive, and full of painful jealousies
Of the Wood-Gods, and even the very trees.
There as he stood, he heard a mournful voice,
Such as once heard, in gentle heart, destroys
All pain but pity: thus the lone voice spake:
"When from this wreathèd tomb shall I awake!
When move in a sweet body fit for life,
And love, and pleasure, and the ruddy strife   40
Of hearts and lips! Ah, miserable me!"
The God, dove-footed, glided silently
Round bush and tree, soft-brushing, in his speed,
The taller grasses and full-flowering weed,
Until he found a palpitating snake,
Bright, and cirque-couchant in a dusky brake.

She was a gordian shape of dazzling hue,
Vermilion-spotted, golden, green, and blue;
Striped like a zebra, freckled like a pard,
Eyed like a peacock, and all crimson barred;   50
And full of silver moons, that, as she breathed,
Dissolved, or brighter shone, or interwreathed
Their lustres with the gloomier tapestries—
So rainbow-sided, touched with miseries,
She seemed, at once, some penanced lady elf,
Some demon's mistress, or the demon's self.
Upon her crest she wore a wannish fire
Sprinkled with stars, like Ariadne's tiar:
Her head was serpent, but ah, bitter-sweet!
She had a woman's mouth with all its pearls complete: 60
And for her eyes: what could such eyes do there
But weep, and weep, that they were born so fair?
As Proserpine still weeps for her Sicilian air.
Her throat was serpent, but the words she spake
Came, as through bubbling honey, for Love's sake,

46 **cirque-couchant** lying coiled up in circles 47 **gordian** intri-
cately coiled 58 **Ariadne's tiar** a crown of stars representing the
constellation into which Ariadne was transformed 63 **Proserpine**
who was carried away from Sicily to live in the lower world

And thus; while Hermes on his pinions lay,
Like a stooped falcon ere he takes his prey.

    "Fair Hermes, crowned with feathers, fluttering light,
    I had a splendid dream of thee last night:
70 I saw thee sitting, on a throne of gold,
    Among the Gods, upon Olympus old,
    The only sad one; for thou didst not hear
    The soft, lute-fingered Muses chaunting clear,
    Nor even Apollo when he sang alone,
    Deaf to his throbbing throat's long, long melodious moan.
    I dreamt I saw thee, robed in purple flakes,
    Break amorous through the clouds, as morning breaks,
    And, swiftly as a bright Phœbean dart,
    Strike for the Cretan isle; and here thou art!
80 Too gentle Hermes, hast thou found the maid?"
    Whereat the star of Lethe not delayed
    His rosy eloquence, and thus inquired:
    "Thou smooth-lipped serpent, surely high inspired!
    Thou beauteous wreath, with melancholy eyes,
    Possess whatever bliss thou canst devise,
    Telling me only where my nymph is fled,—
    Where she doth breathe!" "Bright planet, thou hast said,"
    Returned the snake, "but seal with oaths, fair God!"
    "I swear," said Hermes, "by my serpent rod,
90 And by thine eyes, and by thy starry crown!"
    Light flew his earnest words, among the blossoms blown.
    Then thus again the brilliance feminine:
    "Too frail of heart! for this lost nymph of thine,
    Free as the air, invisibly, she strays
    About these thornless wilds; her pleasant days
    She tastes unseen; unseen her nimble feet
    Leave traces in the grass and flowers sweet;
    From weary tendrils, and bowed branches green,
    She plucks the fruit unseen, she bathes unseen:
100 And by my power is her beauty veiled
    To keep it unaffronted, unassailed
    By the love-glances of unlovely eyes,
    Of Satyrs, Fauns, and bleared Silenus' sighs.

81 **star of Lethe** Hermes, who guided souls of the dead to Lethe
and other rivers of Hades   103 **Silenus** a drunken elderly satyr

Pale grew her immortality, for woe
Of all these lovers, and she grievèd so
I took compassion on her, bade her steep
Her hair in weïrd syrops, that would keep
Her loveliness invisible, yet free
To wander as she loves, in liberty.
Thou shalt behold her, Hermes, thou alone,   110
If thou wilt, as thou swearest, grant my boon!"
Then, once again, the charmèd God began
An oath, and through the serpent's ears it ran
Warm, tremulous, devout, psalterian.
Ravished, she lifted her Circean head,
Blushed a live damask, and swift-lisping said,
"I was a woman, let me have once more
A woman's shape, and charming as before.
I love a youth of Corinth—O the bliss!
Give me my woman's form, and place me where he is.   120
Stoop, Hermes, let me breathe upon thy brow,
And thou shalt see thy sweet nymph even now."
The God on half-shut feathers sank serene,
She breathed upon his eyes, and swift was seen
Of both the guarded nymph near-smiling on the green.
It was no dream; or say a dream it was,
Real are the dreams of Gods, and smoothly pass
Their pleasures in a long immortal dream.
One warm, flushed moment, hovering, it might seem
Dashed by the wood-nymph's beauty, so he burned;   130
Then, lighting on the printless verdure, turned
To the swooned serpent, and with languid arm,
Delicate, put to proof the lythe Caducean charm.
So done, upon the nymph his eyes he bent
Full of adoring tears and blandishment,
And towards her stept: she, like a moon in wane,
Faded before him, cowered, nor could restrain
Her fearful sobs, self-folding like a flower
That faints into itself at evening hour:
But the God fostering her chillèd hand,   140
She felt the warmth, her eyelids opened bland,
And, like new flowers at morning song of bees,

115 **Circean** as if transformed by the sorceress, Circe, who
changed humans into the form of animals   133 **Caducean** of Ca-
duceus, the name of a wand carried by Hermes

Bloomed, and gave up her honey to the lees.
Into the green-recessèd woods they flew;
Nor grew they pale, as mortal lovers do.

Left to herself, the serpent now began
To change; her elfin blood in madness ran,
Her mouth foamed, and the grass, therewith besprent,
Withered at dew so sweet and virulent;
150 Her eyes in torture fixed, and anguish drear,
Hot, glazed, and wide, with lid-lashes all sear,
Flashed phosphor and sharp sparks, without one cooling
    tear.
The colours all inflamed throughout her train,
She writhed about, convulsed with scarlet pain:
A deep volcanian yellow took the place
Of all her milder-moonèd body's grace;
And, as the lava ravishes the mead,
Spoilt all her silver mail, and golden brede;
Made gloom of all her frecklings, streaks and bars,
160 Eclipsed her crescents, and licked up her stars:
So that, in moments few, she was undrest
Of all her sapphires, greens, and amethyst,
And rubious-argent: of all these bereft,
Nothing but pain and ugliness were left.
Still shone her crown; that vanished, also she
Melted and disappeared as suddenly;
And in the air, her new voice luting soft,
Cried, "Lycius! gentle Lycius!"—Borne aloft
With the bright mists about the mountains hoar
170 These words dissolved: Crete's forests heard no more.

Whither fled Lamia, now a lady bright,
A full-born beauty new and exquisite?
She fled into that valley they pass o'er
Who go to Corinth from Cenchreas' shore;
And rested at the foot of those wild hills,
The rugged founts of the Peræan rills,
And of that other ridge whose barren back
Stretches, with all its mist and cloudy rack,
South-westward to Cleone. There she stood
180 About a young bird's flutter from a wood,

158 **brede** woven or braid-like pattern

Fair, on a sloping green of mossy tread,
By a clear pool, wherein she passionèd
To see herself escaped from so sore ills,
While her robes flaunted with the daffodils.

    Ah, happy Lycius!—for she was a maid
More beautiful than ever twisted braid,
Or sighed, or blushed, or on spring-flowered **lea**
Spread a green kirtle to the minstrelsy:
A virgin purest lipped, yet in the lore
Of love deep learned to the red heart's core: 190
Not one hour old, yet of sciential brain
To unperplex bliss from its neighbour pain;
Define their pettish limits, and estrange
Their points of contact, and swift counterchange;
Intrigue with the specious chaos, and dispart
Its most ambiguous atoms with sure art;
As though in Cupid's college she had spent
Sweet days a lovely graduate, still unshent,
And kept his rosy terms in idle languishment.

    Why this fair creature chose so fairily   200
By the wayside to linger, we shall see;
But first 'tis fit to tell how she could muse
And dream, when in the serpent prison-house,
Of all she list, strange or magnificent:
How, ever, where she willed, her spirit went;
Whether to faint Elysium, or where
Down through tress-lifting waves the Nereids **fair**
Wind into Thetis' bower by many a pearly stair;
Or where God Bacchus drains his cups divine,
Stretched out, at ease, beneath a glutinous pine;   210
Or where in Pluto's gardens palatine
Mulciber's columns gleam in far piazzian line.
And sometimes into cities she would send
Her dream, with feast and rioting to blend;
And once, while among mortals dreaming thus,
She saw the young Corinthian Lycius
Charioting foremost in the envious race,

198 **unshent** unspoiled 207 **Nereids** sea nymphs 208 **Thetis a sea**
goddess 211 **palatine** palatial 212 **Mulciber** or Vulcan, **god of**
fire and of the forge

Like a young Jove with calm uneager face,
And fell into a swooning love of him.
220 Now on the moth-time of that evening dim
He would return that way, as well she knew,
To Corinth from the shore; for freshly blew
The eastern soft wind, and his galley now
Grated the quaystones with her brazen prow
In port Cenchreas, from Egina isle
Fresh anchored; whither he had been awhile
To sacrifice to Jove, whose temple there
Waits with high marble doors for blood and incense rare.
Jove heard his vows, and bettered his desire;
230 For by some freakful chance he made retire
From his companions, and set forth to walk,
Perhaps grown wearied of their Corinth talk:
Over the solitary hills he fared,
Thoughtless at first, but ere eve's star appeared
His phantasy was lost, where reason fades,
In the calmed twilight of Platonic shades.
Lamia beheld him coming, near, more near—
Close to her passing, in indifference drear,
His silent sandals swept the mossy green;
240 So neighboured to him, and yet so unseen
She stood: he passed, shut up in mysteries,
His mind wrapped like his mantle, while her eyes
Followed his steps, and her neck regal white
Turned—syllabling thus, "Ah, Lycius bright,
And will you leave me on the hills alone?
Lycius, look back! and be some pity shown."
He did; not with cold wonder fearingly,
But Orpheus-like at an Eurydice;
For so delicious were the words she sung,
250 It seemed he had loved them a whole summer long:
And soon his eyes had drunk her beauty up,
Leaving no drop in the bewildering cup,
And still the cup was full,—while he, afraid
Lest she should vanish ere his lip had paid
Due adoration, thus began to adore;
Her soft look growing coy, she saw his chain so sure:
"Leave thee alone! Look back! Ah, Goddess, see
Whether my eyes can ever turn from thee!
For pity do not this sad heart belie—

Even as thou vanishest so shall I die.   260
Stay! though a Naiad of the rivers, stay!
To thy far wishes will thy streams obey:
Stay! though the greenest woods be thy domain,
Alone they can drink up the morning rain:
Though a descended Pleiad, will not one
Of thine harmonious sisters keep in tune
Thy spheres, and as thy silver proxy shine?
So sweetly to these ravished ears of mine
Came thy sweet greeting, that if thou shouldst fade
Thy memory will waste me to a shade:—   270
For pity do not melt!"—"If I should stay,"
Said Lamia, "here, upon this floor of clay,
And pain my steps upon these flowers too rough,
What canst thou say or do of charm enough
To dull the nice remembrance of my home?
Thou canst not ask me with thee here to roam
Over these hills and vales, where no joy is,—
Empty of immortality and bliss!
Thou art a scholar, Lycius, and must know
That finer spirits cannot breathe below   280
In human climes, and live: Alas! poor youth,
What taste of purer air hast thou to soothe
My essence? What serener palaces,
Where I may all my many senses please,
And by mysterious sleights a hundred thirsts appease?
It cannot be—Adieu!" So said, she rose
Tiptoe with white arms spread. He, sick to lose
The amorous promise of her lone complain,
Swooned, murmuring of love, and pale with pain.
The cruel lady, without any show   290
Of sorrow for her tender favourite's woe,
But rather, if her eyes could brighter be,
With brighter eyes and slow amenity,
Put her new lips to his, and gave afresh
The life she had so tangled in her mesh:
And as he from one trance was wakening
Into another, she began to sing,
Happy in beauty, life, and love, and every thing,
A song of love, too sweet for earthly lyres,

261 **Naiad** water nymph 265 **Pleiad** one of the seven nymphs
changed into the constellation Pleiades

300 While, like held breath, the stars drew in their panting fires.
And then she whispered in such trembling tone,
As those who, safe together met alone
For the first time through many anguished days,
Use other speech than looks; bidding him raise
His drooping head, and clear his soul of doubt,
For that she was a woman, and without
Any more subtle fluid in her veins
Than throbbing blood, and that the self-same pains
Inhabited her frail-strung heart as his.

310 And next she wondered how his eyes could miss
Her face so long in Corinth, where, she said,
She dwelt but half retired, and there had led
Days happy as the gold coin could invent
Without the aid of love; yet in content
Till she saw him, as once she passed him by,
Where 'gainst a column he leant thoughtfully
At Venus' temple porch, 'mid baskets heaped
Of amorous herbs and flowers, newly reaped
Late on that eve, as 'twas the night before

320 The Adonian feast; whereof she saw no more,
But wept alone those days, for why should she adore?
Lycius from death awoke into amaze,
To see her still, and singing so sweet lays;
Then from amaze into delight he fell
To hear her whisper woman's lore so well;
And every word she spake enticed him on
To unperplexed delight and pleasure known.
Let the mad poets say whate'er they please
Of the sweets of Fairies, Peris, Goddesses,

330 There is not such a treat among them all,
Haunters of cavern, lake, and waterfall,
As a real woman, lineal indeed
From Pyrrha's pebbles or old Adam's seed.
Thus gentle Lamia judged, and judged aright,
That Lycius could not love in half a fright,
So threw the goddess off, and won his heart
More pleasantly by playing woman's part,
With no more awe than what her beauty gave,
That, while it smote, still guaranteed to save.

333 **Pyrrha's pebbles** like Noah, Pyrrha survived a great flood.
Afterwards she cast stones behind her which sprang up as **women**

Lycius to all made eloquent reply,   340
Marrying to every word a twinborn sigh;
And last, pointing to Corinth, asked her sweet,
If 'twas too far that night for her soft feet.
The way was short, for Lamia's eagerness
Made, by a spell, the triple league decrease
To a few paces; not at all surmised
By blinded Lycius, so in her comprized.
They passed the city gates, he knew not how,
So noiseless, and he never thought to know.

As men talk in a dream, so Corinth all,   350
Throughout her palaces imperial,
And all her populous streets and temples lewd,
Muttered, like tempest in the distance brewed,
To the wide-spreaded night above her towers.
Men, women, rich and poor, in the cool hours,
Shuffled their sandals o'er the pavement white,
Companioned or alone; while many a light
Flared, here and there, from wealthy festivals,
And threw their moving shadows on the walls,
Or found them clustered in the corniced shade   360
Of some arched temple door, or dusky colonnade.

Muffling his face, of greeting friends in fear,
Her fingers he pressed hard, as one came near
With curled gray beard, sharp eyes, and smooth bald crown,
Slow-stepped, and robed in philosophic gown:
Lycius shrank closer, as they met and past,
Into his mantle, adding wings to haste,
While hurried Lamia trembled: "Ah," said he,
"Why do you shudder, love, so ruefully?
Why does your tender palm dissolve in dew?"—   370
"I'm wearied," said fair Lamia: "tell me who
Is that old man? I cannot bring to mind
His features:—Lycius! wherefore did you blind
Yourself from his quick eyes?" Lycius replied,
" 'Tis Apollonius sage, my trusty guide
And good instructor; but to-night he seems
The ghost of folly haunting my sweet dreams."

While yet he spake they had arrived before
A pillared porch, with lofty portal door,

380 Where hung a silver lamp, whose phosphor glow
Reflected in the slabbèd steps below,
Mild as a star in water; for so new,
And so unsullied was the marble's hue,
So through the crystal polish, liquid fine,
Ran the dark veins, that none but feet divine
Could e'er have touched there. Sounds Æolian
Breathed from the hinges, as the ample span
Of the wide doors disclosed a place unknown
Some time to any, but those two alone,
390 And a few Persian mutes, who that same year
Were seen about the markets: none knew where
They could inhabit; the most curious
Were foiled, who watched to trace them to their house:
And but the flitter-wingèd verse must tell,
For truth's sake, what woe afterwards befel,
'Twould humour many a heart to leave them thus,
Shut from the busy world of more incredulous.

PART II

Love in a hut, with water and a crust,
Is—Love, forgive us!—cinders, ashes, dust;
Love in a palace is perhaps at last
More grievous torment than a hermit's fast:—
That is a doubtful tale from faery land,
Hard for the non-elect to understand.
Had Lycius lived to hand his story down,
He might have given the moral a fresh frown,
Or clenched it quite: but too short was their bliss
10 To breed distrust and hate, that make the soft voice hiss.
Besides, there, nightly, with terrific glare,
Love, jealous grown of so complete a pair,
Hovered and buzzed his wings, with fearful roar,
Above the lintel of their chamber door,
And down the passage cast a glow upon the floor.

For all this came a ruin: side by side
They were enthronèd, in the even tide,

386 **Aeolian** kind of harp played by the wind 6 **non-elect those**
not yet chosen by fate to experience the torments of love

Upon a couch, near to a curtaining
Whose airy texture, from a golden string,
Floated into the room, and let appear   20
Unveiled the summer heaven, blue and clear,
Betwixt two marble shafts:—there they reposed,
Where use had made it sweet, with eyelids closed,
Saving a tythe which love still open kept,
That they might see each other while they almost slept;
When from the slope side of a suburb hill,
Deafening the swallow's twitter, came a thrill
Of trumpets—Lycius started—the sounds fled,
But left a thought a-buzzing in his head.
For the first time, since he first harboured in   30
That purple-linèd palace of sweet sin,
His spirit passed beyond its golden bourn
Into the noisy world almost forsworn.
The lady, ever watchful, penetrant,
Saw this with pain, so arguing a want
Of something more, more than her empery
Of joys; and she began to moan and sigh
Because he mused beyond her, knowing well
That but a moment's thought is passion's passing bell.
"Why do you sigh, fair creature?" whispered he: 40
"Why do you think?" returned she tenderly:
"You have deserted me;—where am I now?
Not in your heart while care weighs on your brow:
No, no, you have dismissed me; and I go
From your breast houseless: ay, it must be so."
He answered, bending to her open eyes,
Where he was mirrored small in paradise,
"My silver planet, both of eve and morn!
Why will you plead yourself so sad forlorn,
While I am striving how to fill my heart   50
With deeper crimson, and a double smart?
How to entangle, trammel up and snare
Your soul in mine, and labyrinth you there
Like the hid scent in an unbudded rose?
Ay, a sweet kiss—you see your mighty woes.
My thoughts! shall I unveil them? Listen then!
What mortal hath a prize, that other men

24 **tythe** a tenth part 32 **bourn** domain 36 **empery** empire

May be confounded and abashed withal,
But lets it sometimes pace abroad majestical,
60 And triumph, as in thee I should rejoice
Amid the hoarse alarm of Corinth's voice.
Let my foes choke, and my friends shout afar,
While through the throngèd streets your bridal car
Wheels round its dazzling spokes."—The lady's cheek
Trembled; she nothing said, but, pale and meek,
Arose and knelt before him, wept a rain
Of sorrows at his words; at last with pain
Beseeching him, the while his hand she wrung,
To change his purpose. He thereat was stung,
70 Perverse, with stronger fancy to reclaim
Her wild and timid nature to his aim:
Besides, for all his love, in self despite
Against his better self, he took delight
Luxurious in her sorrows, soft and new.
His passion, cruel grown, took on a hue
Fierce and sanguineous as 'twas possible
In one whose brow had no dark veins to swell.
Fine was the mitigated fury, like
Apollo's presence when in act to strike
80 The serpent—Ha, the serpent! certes, she
Was none. She burnt, she loved the tyranny,
And, all subdued, consented to the hour
When to the bridal he should lead his paramour.
Whispering in midnight silence, said the youth,
"Sure some sweet name thou hast, though, by my truth,
I have not asked it, ever thinking thee
Not mortal, but of heavenly progeny,
As still I do. Hast any mortal name,
Fit appellation for this dazzling frame?
90 Or friends or kinsfolk on the citied earth,
To share our marriage feast and nuptial mirth?"
"I have no friends," said Lamia, "no, not one;
My presence in wide Corinth hardly known:
My parents' bones are in their dusty urns
Sepulchred, where no kindled incense burns,
Seeing all their luckless race are dead, save me,
And I neglect the holy rite for thee.
Even as you list invite your many guests;
But if, as now it seems, your vision rests

With any pleasure on me, do not bid   100
Old Apollonius—from him keep me hid."
Lycius, perplexed at words so blind and blank,
Made close inquiry; from whose touch she shrank,
Feigning a sleep; and he to the dull shade
Of deep sleep in a moment was betrayed.

It was the custom then to bring away
The bride from home at blushing shut of day,
Veiled, in a chariot, heralded along
By strewn flowers, torches, and a marriage song,
With other pageants: but this fair unknown   110
Had not a friend. So being left alone,
(Lycius was gone to summon all his kin)
And knowing surely she could never win
His foolish heart from its mad pompousness,
She set herself, high-thoughted, how to dress
The misery in fit magnificence.
She did so, but 'tis doubtful how and whence
Came, and who were her subtle servitors.
About the halls, and to and from the doors,
There was a noise of wings, till in short space   120
The glowing banquet-room shone with wide-archèd grace.
A haunting music, sole perhaps and lone
Supportress of the faery-roof, made moan
Throughout, as fearful the whole charm might fade.
Fresh carvèd cedar, mimicking a glade
Of palm and plantain, met from either side,
High in the midst, in honour of the bride:
Two palms and then two plantains, and so on,
From either side their stems branched one to one
All down the aislèd place; and beneath all   130
There ran a stream of lamps straight on from wall to wall.
So canopied, lay an untasted feast
Teeming with odours. Lamia, regal drest,
Silently paced about, and as she went,
In pale contented sort of discontent,
Missioned her viewless servants to enrich
The fretted splendour of each nook and niche.
Between the tree-stems, marbled plain at first,
Came jasper pannels; then, anon, there burst
Forth creeping imagery of slighter trees,   140

And with the larger wove in small intricacies.
Approving all, she faded at self-will,
And shut the chamber up, close, hushed and still,
Complete and ready for the revels rude,
When dreadful guests would come to spoil her soilitude.

The day appeared, and all the gossip rout.
O senseless Lycius! Madman! wherefore flout
The silent-blessing fate, warm cloistered hours,
And show to common eyes these secret bowers?
150 The herd approached; each guest, with busy brain,
Arriving at the portal, gazed amain,
And entered marveling: for they knew the street,
Remembered it from childhood all complete
Without a gap, yet ne'er before had seen
That royal porch, that high-built fair demesne;
So in they hurried all, mazed, curious and keen:
Save one, who looked thereon with eye severe,
And with calm-planted steps walked in austere;
'Twas Apollonius: something too he laughed,
160 As though some knotty problem, that had daft
His patient thought, had now begun to thaw,
And solve and melt:—'twas just as he foresaw.

He met within the murmurous vestibule
His young disciple. " 'Tis no common rule,
Lycius," said he, "for uninvited guest
To force himself upon you, and infest
With an unbidden presence the bright throng
Of younger friends; yet must I do this wrong,
And you forgive me." Lycius blushed, and led
170 The old man through the inner doors broad-spread;
With reconciling words and courteous mien
Turning into sweet milk the sophist's spleen.

Of wealthy lustre was the banquet-room,
Filled with pervading brilliance and perfume:
Before each lucid pannel fuming stood
A censer fed with myrrh and spicèd wood,
Each by a sacred tripod held aloft,
Whose slender feet wide-swerved upon the soft
160 daft eluded

Wool-woofèd carpets: fifty wreaths of smoke
From fifty censers their light voyage took   180
To the high roof, still mimicked as they rose
Along the mirrored walls by twin-clouds odorous.
Twelve spherèd tables, by silk seats insphered,
High as the level of a man's breast reared
On libbard's paws, upheld the heavy gold
Of cups and goblets, and the store thrice told
Of Ceres' horn, and, in huge vessels, wine
Come from the gloomy tun with merry shine.
Thus loaded with a feast the tables stood,
Each shrining in the midst the image of a God.   190

   When in an antichamber every guest
Had felt the cold full sponge to pleasure pressed,
My minist'ring slaves, upon his hands and feet,
And fragrant oils with ceremony meet
Poured on his hair, they all moved to the feast
In white robes, and themselves in order placed
Around the silken couches, wondering
Whence all this mighty cost and blaze of wealth could
     spring.

   Soft went the music the soft air along,
While fluent Greek a voweled undersong   200
Kept up among the guests, discoursing low
At first, for scarcely was the wine at flow;
But when the happy vintage touched their brains,
Louder they talk, and louder come the strains
Of powerful instruments:—the gorgeous dyes,
The space, the splendour of the draperies,
The roof of awful richness, nectarous cheer,
Beautiful slaves, and Lamia's self, appear,
Now, when the wine has done its rosy deed,
And every soul from human trammels freed,   210
No more so strange; for merry wine, sweet wine,
Will make Elysian shades not too fair, too divine.
Soon was God Bacchus at meridian height;
Flushed were their cheeks, and bright eyes double bright:
Garlands of every green, and every scent

185 libbard leopard **187 Ceres' horn** horn-shaped vessel over-
flowing with products of the harvest

From vales deflowered, or forest-trees branch-rent,
In baskets of bright osiered gold were brought
High as the handles heaped, to suit the thought
Of every guest; that each, as he did please,
220 Might fancy-fit his brows, silk-pillowed at his ease.

What wreath for Lamia? What for Lycius?
What for the sage, old Apollonius?
Upon her aching forehead be there hung
The leaves of willow and of adder's tongue;
And for the youth, quick, let us strip for him
The thyrsus, that his watching eyes may swim
Into forgetfulness; and, for the sage,
Let spear-grass and the spiteful thistle wage
War on his temples. Do not all charms fly
230 At the mere touch of cold philosophy?
There was an awful rainbow once in heaven:
We know her woof, her texture; she is given
In the dull catalogue of common things.
Philosophy will clip an Angel's wings,
Conquer all mysteries by rule and line,
Empty the haunted air, and gnomèd mine—
Unweave a rainbow, as it erewhile made
The tender-personed Lamia melt into a shade.

By her glad Lycius sitting, in chief place,
240 Scarce saw in all the room another face,
Till, checking his love trance, a cup he took
Full brimmed, and opposite sent forth a look
'Cross the broad table, to beseech a glance
From his old teacher's wrinkled countenance,
And pledge him. The bald-head philosopher
Had fixed his eye, without a twinkle of stir
Full on the alarmèd beauty of the bride,
Brow-beating her fair form, and troubling her sweet pride.
Lycius then pressed her hand, with devout touch,
250 As pale it lay upon the rosy couch:
'Twas icy, and the cold ran through his veins;
Then sudden it grew hot, and all the pains

217 **osiered** woven as willow branches are woven 224 **adder's tongue** kind of fern 226 **thyrsus** wand wreathed with ivy 230 **philosophy** systematic knowledge, including natural science

Of an unnatural heat shot to his heart.
"Lamia, what means this? Wherefore dost thou start?
Know'st thou that man?" Poor Lamia answered not.
He gazed into her eyes, and not a jot
Owned they the lovelorn piteous appeal:
More, more he gazed: his human senses reel:
Some hungry spell that loveliness absorbs;
There was no recognition in those orbs.   260
"Lamia!" he cried—and no soft-toned reply.
The many heard, and the loud revelry
Grew hush; the stately music no more breathes;
The myrtle sickened in a thousand wreaths.
By faint degrees, voice, lute, and pleasure ceased;
A deadly silence step by step increased,
Until it seemed a horrid presence there,
And not a man but felt the terror in his hair.
"Lamia!" he shrieked; and nothing but the shriek
With its sad echo did the silence break.   270
"Begone, foul dream!" he cried, gazing again
In the bride's face, where now no azure vein
Wandered on fair-spaced temples; no soft bloom
Misted the cheek; no passion to illume
The deep-recessèd vision:—all was blight;
Lamia, no longer fair, there sat a deadly white.
"Shut, shut those juggling eyes, thou ruthless man!
Turn them aside, wretch! or the righteous ban
Of all the Gods, whose dreadful images
Here represent their shadowy presences,   280
May pierce them on the sudden with the thorn
Of painful blindness; leaving thee forlorn,
In trembling dotage to the feeblest fright
Of conscience, for their long offended might,
For all thine impious proud-heart sophistries,
Unlawful magic, and enticing lies.
Corinthians! look upon that gray-beard wretch!
Mark how, possessed, his lashless eyelids stretch
Around his demon eyes! Corinthians, see!
My sweet bride withers at their potency."   290
"Fool!" said the sophist, in an under-tone
Gruff with contempt; which a death-nighing moan
From Lycius answered, as heart-struck and lost,
He sank supine beside the aching ghost.

"Fool! Fool!" repeated he, while his eyes still
Relented not, nor moved; "from every ill
Of life have I preserved thee to this day,
And shall I see thee made a serpent's prey?"
Then Lamia breathed death breath; the sophist's eye,
300 Like a sharp spear, went through her utterly,
Keen, cruel, perceant, stinging: she, as well
As her weak hand could any meaning tell,
Motioned him to be silent; vainly so,
He looked and looked again a level—No!
"A serpent!" echoed he; no sooner said,
Than with a frightful scream she vanishèd:
And Lycius' arms were empty of delight,
As were his limbs of life, from that same night.
On the high couch he lay!—his friends came round—
310 Supported him—no pulse, or breath they found,
And, in its marriage robe, the heavy body wound.

1819   *1820*

311 **In Keats' edition, the following extract is appended as a note:**
"Philostratus, in his fourth book *de Vita Apollonii*, hath a memorable instance in this kind, which I may not omit, of one Menippus Lycius, a young man twenty-five years of age, that going betwixt Cenchreas and Corinth, met such a phantasm in the habit of a fair gentlewoman, which, taking him by the hand, carried him home to her house, in the suburbs of Corinth, and told him she was a Phœnician by birth, and if he would tarry with her, he should hear her sing and play, and drink such wine as never any drank, and no man should molest him; but she, being fair and lovely, would live and die with him, that was fair and lovely to behold. The young man, a philosopher, otherwise staid and discreet, able to moderate his passions, though not this of love, tarried with her a while to his great content, and at last married her, to whose wedding, amongst other guests, came Apollonius; who, by some probable conjectures, found her out to be a serpent, a lamia; and that all her furniture was, like Tantalus' gold, described by Homer, no substance but mere illusions. When she saw herself descried, she wept, and desired Apollonius to be silent, but he would not be moved, and thereupon she, plate, house, and all that was in it, vanished in an instant: many thousands took notice of this fact, for it was done in the midst of Greece." Burton's *Anatomy of Melancholy, Part 3. Sect. 2.*

To Autumn

[handwritten: death presented in images of autumn]

SEASON of mists and mellow fruitfulness,
  Close bosom-friend of the maturing sun;
Conspiring with him how to load and bless
  With fruit the vines that round the thatch-eves run;
To bend with apples the mossed cottage-trees,
  And fill all fruit with ripeness to the core;
    To swell the gourd, and plump the hazel shells
  With a sweet kernel; to set budding more,
And still more, later flowers for the bees,
Until they think warm days will never cease,   10
    For Summer has o'er-brimmed their clammy cells.

Who hath not seen thee oft amid thy store?
  Sometimes whoever seeks abroad may find
Thee sitting careless on a granary floor,
  Thy hair soft-lifted by the winnowing wind;
Or on a half-reaped furrow sound asleep,
  Drowsed with the fume of poppies, while thy hook
    Spares the next swath and all its twinèd flowers:
And sometimes like a gleaner thou dost keep
  Steady thy laden head across a brook;   20
  Or by a cyder-press, with patient look,
    Thou watchest the last oozings hours by hours.

Where are the songs of Spring? Ay, where are they?
  Think not of them, thou hast thy music too,—
While barrèd clouds bloom the soft-dying day,
  And touch the stubble-plains with rosy hue;
Then in a wailful choir the small gnats mourn
  Among the river sallows, borne aloft
    Or sinking as the light wind lives or dies;
And full-grown lambs loud bleat from hilly bourn;   30
  Hedge-crickets sing; and now with treble soft
  The red-breast whistles from a garden-croft;
    And gathering swallows twitter in the skies.

1819   *1820*

Lines supposed to have been addressed to Fanny Brawne

THIS living hand, now warm and capable
Of earnest grasping, would, if it were cold
And in the icy silence of the tomb,
So haunt thy days and chill thy dreaming nights
That thou wouldst wish thine own heart dry of blood
So in my veins red life might stream again,
And thou be conscience-calmed—see here it is—
I hold it towards you.

1820(?)   *1898*

SONNETS

I

"HOW MANY BARDS"

How many bards gild the lapses of time!
　　A few of them have ever been the food
　　Of my delighted fancy,—I could brood
Over their beauties, earthly, or sublime:
And often, when I sit me down to rhyme,
　　These will in throngs before my mind intrude:
　　But no confusion, no disturbance rude
Do they occasion; 'tis a pleasing chime.
So the unnumbered sounds that evening store;
The songs of birds—the whisp'ring of the leaves—　　10
　　The voice of waters—the great bell that heaves
With solemn sound,—and thousand others more,
　　That distance of recognizance bereaves,
Make pleasing music, and not wild uproar.
1816　　　　　　　　　　　　　　　　　　　　　　*1817*

II

ON FIRST LOOKING INTO CHAPMAN'S
HOMER

Much have I travelled in the realms of gold,
　　And many goodly states and kingdoms seen;
　　Round many western islands have I been
Which bards in fealty to Apollo hold.
Oft of one wide expanse had I been told
　　That deep-browed Homer ruled as his demesne;　　20
　　Yet did I never breathe its pure serene
Till I heard Chapman speak out loud and bold:
Then felt I like some watcher of the skies
　　When a new planet swims into his ken;
Or like stout Cortez when with eagle eyes
　　He stared at the Pacific—and all his men
Looked at each other with a wild surmise—
　　Silent, upon a peak in Darien.
1816　　　　　　　　　　　　　　　　　　　　　　*1816*

18 **Apollo** god to whom poets owe allegiance 22 **Chapman** a seventeenth century translator 25 **Cortez** an explorer, but not the actual discoverer of the Pacific, which was first seen from **Darien** by **Balboa**

105

III

"KEEN, FITFUL GUSTS"

KEEN, fitful gusts are whisp'ring here and there
　　Among the bushes half leafless, and dry;
　　The stars look very cold about the sky,
And I have many miles on foot to fare.
Yet feel I little of the cool bleak air,
　　Or of the dead leaves rustling drearily,
　　Or of those silver lamps that burn on high,
Or of the distance from home's pleasant lair:
For I am brimfull of the friendliness
10　　That in a little cottage I have found;
Of fair-haired Milton's eloquent distress,
　　And all his love for gentle Lycid drowned;
Of lovely Laura in her light green dress,
　　And faithful Petrarch gloriously crowned.
1816   *1817*

IV

TO MY BROTHERS

SMALL, busy flames play through the fresh laid coals,
　　And their faint cracklings o'er our silence creep
　　Like whispers of the household gods that keep
A gentle empire o'er fraternal souls.
And while, for rhymes, I search around the poles,
20　　Your eyes are fixed, as in poetic sleep,
　　Upon the lore so voluble and deep,
That aye at fall of night our care condoles.
This is your birth-day Tom, and I rejoice
　　That thus it passes smoothly, quietly.
Many such eves of gently whisp'ring noise
　　May we together pass, and calmly try
What are this world's true joys,—ere the great voice,
　　From its fair face, shall bid our spirits fly.
1816   *1817*

10 **cottage** home of Leigh Hunt 12 **Lycid** in Milton's elegy "Ly-
cidas" 13 **Laura** beloved of the Italian poet Petrarch (1303-
74)

V

ON THE GRASSHOPPER AND CRICKET

THE poetry of earth is never dead:
  When all the birds are faint with the hot sun,
  And hide in cooling trees, a voice will run
From hedge to hedge about the new-mown mead;
That is the Grasshopper's—he takes the lead
  In summer luxury,—he has never done
  With his delights; for when tired out with fun
He rests at ease beneath some pleasant weed.
The poetry of earth is ceasing never:
  On a lone winter evening, when the frost   10
    Has wrought a silence, from the stove there shrills
The Cricket's song, in warmth increasing ever,
  And seems to one in drowsiness half lost,
    The Grasshopper's among some grassy hills.

1816   *1817*

VI

"AFTER DARK VAPOURS"

AFTER dark vapours have oppressed our plains
  For a long dreary season, comes a day
  Born of the gentle South, and clears away
From the sick heavens all unseemly stains.
The anxious month, relievèd of its pains,
  Takes as a long-lost right the feel of May;   20
  The eyelids with the passing coolness play
Like rose leaves with the drip of summer rains.
The calmest thoughts come round us—as of leaves
  Budding—fruit ripening in stillness—autumn suns
Smiling at eve upon the quiet sheaves—
Sweet Sappho's cheek—a smiling infant's breath—
  The gradual sand that through an hour-glass runs—
A woodland rivulet—a Poet's death.

1817   *1817*

VII

TO LEIGH HUNT, ESQ.

GLORY and loveliness have passed away;
   For if we wander out in early morn,
   No wreathèd incense do we see upborne
Into the east, to meet the smiling day:
No crowd of nymphs soft voiced and young, and gay,,
   In woven baskets bringing ears of corn,
   Roses, and pinks, and violets, to adorn
The shrine of Flora in her early May.
But there are left delights as high as these,
10   And I shall ever bless my destiny,
That in a time, when under pleasant trees
   Pan is no longer sought, I feel a free,
A leafy luxury, seeing I could please
   With these poor offerings, a man like thee.
1817   *1817*

VIII

ON SEEING THE ELGIN MARBLES

MY spirit is too weak—mortality
   Weighs heavily on me like unwilling sleep,
   And each imagined pinnacle and steep
Of godlike hardship, tells me I must die
Like a sick Eagle looking at the sky.
20   Yet 'tis a gentle luxury to weep
   That I have not the cloudy winds to keep,
Fresh for the opening of the morning's eye.
Such dim-conceivèd glories of the brain
   Bring round the heart an undescribable feud;
So do these wonders a most dizzy pain,
   That mingles Grecian grandeur with the rude
Wasting of old Time—with a billowy main—
   A sun—a shadow of a magnitude.
1817   *1817*

14 **offerings** volume of poems dedicated to Hunt 25 **wonders** ancient sculptures brought to England by Lord Elgin from the Parthenon in Greece

IX

ON THE SEA

IT keeps eternal whisperings around
  Desolate shores, and with its mighty swell
  Gluts twice ten thousand Caverns, till the spell
Of Hecate leaves them their old shadowy sound.
Often 'tis in such gentle temper found,
  That scarcely will the very smallest shell
  Be moved for days from where it sometime fell,
When last the winds of Heaven were unbound.
Oh ye! who have your eye-balls vexed and tired,
  Feast them upon the wideness of the Sea;   10
    Oh ye! whose ears are dinned with uproar rude,
    Or fed too much with cloying melody—
      Sit ye near some old cavern's mouth, and brood
Until ye start, as if the sea-nymphs quired!
1817   *1817*

X

TO MRS. REYNOLDS'S CAT

CAT! who hast passed thy grand climacteric,
  How many mice and rats hast in thy days
  Destroyed?—How many tit bits stolen? Gaze
With those bright languid segments green, and prick
Those velvet ears—but pr'ythee do not stick
  Thy latent talons in me—and upraise   20
  Thy gentle mew—and tell me all thy frays
Of fish and mice, and rats and tender chick.
Nay, look not down, nor lick thy dainty wrists—
  For all the wheezy asthma,—and for all
Thy tail's tip is nicked off—and though the fists
  Of many a maid have given thee many a maul,
Still is that fur as soft as when the lists
  In youth thou enter'dst on glass bottled wall.
1818   *1830*

Title **To . . . Cat** a parody of the Petrarchan sonnet-form. Cf.
Gray's "Ode on the Death of a Favourite Cat" 15 **grand climac-
teric** in humans, the supposedly hazardous sixty-third year of life
23 **look not down** don't be ashamed

XI

ON SITTING DOWN TO READ KING LEAR
ONCE AGAIN

O GOLDEN tongued Romance, with serene lute!
    Fair plumèd Syren, Queen of far-away!
    Leave melodizing on this wintry day,
Shut up thine olden pages, and be mute:
Adieu! for, once again, the fierce dispute
    Betwixt damnation and impassioned clay
    Must I burn through; once more humbly assay
The bitter-sweet of this Shakespearian fruit:
Chief Poet! and ye clouds of Albion,
    Begetters of our deep eternal theme!
When through the old oak Forest I am gone,
    Let me not wander in a barren dream,
But, when I am consumèd in the fire,
Give me new Phœnix wings to fly at my desire.

1818   *1848*

XII

"WHEN I HAVE FEARS"

WHEN I have fears that I may cease to be
    Before my pen has gleaned my teeming brain,
Before high-pilèd books, in charactery,
    Hold like rich garners the full ripened grain;
When I behold, upon the night's starred face,
    Huge cloudy symbols of a high romance,
And think that I may never live to trace
    Their shadows, with the magic hand of chance;
And when I feel, fair creature of an hour,
    That I shall never look upon thee more,
Never have relish in the faery power
    Of unreflecting love!—then on the shore
Of the wide world I stand alone, and think
Till love and fame to nothingness do sink.

1818   *1848*

1 **Romance** perhaps Spenser's *Faerie Queene*   14 **Phoenix** mythical bird which regains vitality by being consumed in fire

XIII

TO A LADY SEEN FOR A FEW MOMENTS
AT VAUXHALL

TIME's sea hath been five years at its slow ebb,
  Long hours have to and fro let creep the sand,
Since I was tangled in thy beauty's web,
  And snared by the ungloving of thine hand.
And yet I never look on midnight sky,
  But I behold thine eyes' well memoried light;
I cannot look upon the rose's dye,
  But to thy cheek my soul doth take its flight;
I cannot look on any budding flower,
  But my fond ear, in fancy at thy lips   10
And hearkening for a love-sound, doth devour
  Its sweets in the wrong sense:—Thou dost eclipse
Every delight with sweet remembering,
And grief unto my darling joys dost bring.
1818   *1844*

XIV

TO HOMER

STANDING aloof in giant ignorance,
  Of thee I hear and of the Cyclades,
As one who sits ashore and longs perchance
  To visit dolphin-coral in deep seas.
So thou wast blind!—but then the veil was rent,
  For Jove uncurtained Heaven to let thee live,   20
And Neptune made for thee a spumy tent,
  And Pan made sing for thee his forest-hive;
Aye on the shores of darkness there is light,
  And precipices show untrodden green,
There is a budding morrow in midnight,
  There is a triple sight in blindness keen;
Such seeing hadst thou, as it once befel
To Dian, Queen of Earth, and Heaven, and Hell.
1818   *1848*

2 **sand** in an hour-glass 14 **darling** best-loved 16 **Cyclades**
Aegean islands 20 **live** be alive by means of imaginative vision

XV

"WHY DID I LAUGH TO-NIGHT?"

WHY did I laugh to-night? No voice will tell:
    No God, no Demon of severe response,
Deigns to reply from heaven or from Hell.
    Then to my human heart I turn at once.
Heart! Thou and I are here sad and alone;
    I say, why did I laugh! O mortal pain!
O Darkness! Darkness! ever must I moan,
    To question Heaven and Hell and Heart in vain.
Why did I laugh? I know this Being's lease,
10   My fancy to its utmost blisses spreads;
Yet would I on this very midnight cease,
    And the world's gaudy ensigns see in shreds;
Verse, Fame, and Beauty are intense indeed,
But Death intenser—Death is Life's high meed.
1819   *1848*

XVI

"BRIGHT STAR"

BRIGHT star! would I were steadfast as thou art—
    Not in lone splendour hung aloft the night
And watching, with eternal lids apart,
    Like nature's patient, sleepless Eremite,
The moving waters at their priestlike task
20   Of pure ablution round earth's human shores,
Or gazing on the new soft-fallen mask
    Of snow upon the mountains and the moors—
No—yet still steadfast, still unchangeable,
    Pillowed upon my fair love's ripening breast,
To feel for ever its soft fall and swell,
    Awake for ever in a sweet unrest,
Still, still to hear her tender-taken breath,
And so live ever—or else swoon to death.
1819   *1848*

12 **ensigns** representing the "utmost blisses" (line 10) yet to be enjoyed in his "lease" of life 18 **Eremite** a hermit, the moon

XVII

TO SLEEP

O soft embalmer of the still midnight,
   Shutting, with careful fingers and benign,
Our gloom-pleased eyes, embowered from the light,
   Enshaded in forgetfulness divine;
O soothest Sleep! if so it please thee, close,
   In midst of this thine hymn, my willing eyes,
Or wait the amen, ere thy poppy throws
   Around my bed its lulling charities;
Then save me, or the passèd day will shine
Upon my pillow, breeding many woes;   10
   Save me from curious conscience, that still lords
Its strength for darkness, burrowing like a mole;
   Turn the key deftly in the oilèd wards,
And seal the hushèd casket of my soul.
1819   *1848*

XVIII

ON FAME

Fame, like a wayward Girl, will still be coy
   To those who woo her with too slavish knees,
But makes surrender to some thoughtless Boy,
   And dotes the more upon a heart at ease;
She is a Gipsey, will not speak to those
   Who have not learnt to be content without her;   20
A Jilt, whose ear was never whispered close,
   Who thinks they scandal her who talk about her;
A very Gipsey is she, Nilus-born,
   Sister-in-law to jealous Potiphar;
Ye love-sick Bards! repay her scorn for scorn,
   Ye Artists lovelorn, madmen that ye are!
Make your best bow to her and bid adieu,
Then, if she likes it, she will follow you.
1819   *1837*

3 **embowered** sheltered 5 **soothest** most soothing 13 **wards** parts
of a lock 23 **Nilus** gipsies were said to have come from Egypt

XIX

ON FAME

You cannot eat your cake and have it too.—Proverb.

How fevered is the man, who cannot look
　　Upon his mortal days with temperate blood,
Who vexes all the leaves of his life's book,
　　And robs his fair name of its maidenhood;
It is as if the rose should pluck herself,
　　Or the ripe plum finger its misty bloom,
As if a Naiad, like a meddling elf,
　　Should darken her pure grot with muddy gloom:
But the rose leaves herself upon the briar,
10　　For winds to kiss and grateful bees to feed,
And the ripe plum still wears its dim attire,
　　　　The undisturbèd lake has crystal space,
　　　　Why then should man, teasing the world for grace,
　　Spoil his salvation for a fierce miscreed?
1819　　　　　　　　　　　　　　　　　　*1848*

XX

"THE DAY IS GONE"

The day is gone, and all its sweets are gone!
　　Sweet voice, sweet lips, soft hand, and softer breast,
Warm breath, light whisper, tender semi-tone,
　　Bright eyes, accomplished shape, and lang'rous waist!
Faded the flower and all its budded charms,
20　　Faded the sight of beauty from my eyes,
Faded the shape of beauty from my arms,
　　Faded the voice, warmth, whiteness, paradise—
Vanished unseasonably at shut of eve,
　　When the dusk holiday—or holinight
Of fragrant-curtained love begins to weave
　　The woof of darkness thick, for hid delight;
But, as I've read love's missal through to-day,
He'll let me sleep, seeing I fast and pray.
1819　　　　　　　　　　　　　　　　　　*1848*

14 **miscreed** mistaken creed　27 **missal** mass-book or prayer-book

BIBLIOGRAPHY

LETTERS AND COMPLETE WORKS

The Poetical Works of John Keats, edited by H. W. Garrod, Oxford, 1939.

The Letters of John Keats, edited by Hyder E. Rollins, Cambridge, Massachusetts, 2 vols., 1958.

BIOGRAPHIES

Bate, Walter J., *John Keats,* Cambridge, Massachusetts, 1963.

Colvin, Sidney, *John Keats,* New York, 1917.

Ward, Aileen, *John Keats: The Making of a Poet,* New York, 1963.

CRITICAL STUDIES

Arnold, Matthew, *Essays in Criticism, Second Series,* London, 1888.

Bate, Walter J., (ed.), *Keats: A Collection of Critical Essays,* Englewood Cliffs, New Jersey, 1964.

Bloom, Harold, *The Visionary Company,* New York, 1961; New York, 1965.

Bush, Douglas, *Mythology and the Romantic Tradition,* Cambridge, Massachusetts, 1937.

Finney, Claude L., *The Evolution of Keats's Poetry,* Cambridge, Massachusetts, 2 vols., 1936.

Fogle, Richard H., *The Imagery of Keats and Shelley,* Chapel Hill, North Carolina, 1949.

Ford, George H., *Keats and the Victorians,* New Haven, 1944.

Ford, Newell F., *The Prefigurative Imagination of John Keats,* Stanford, 1951.

Murry, J. Middleton, *Keats and Shakespeare,* Oxford, 1925.

Ridley, M. R., *Keats's Craftsmanship,* Oxford, 1933.

Thorpe, Clarence D., *The Mind of John Keats,* New York, 1926.

Wasserman, Earl, *The Finer Tone,* Baltimore, 1953.